TO LOVE AND GO ON LOVING

To Love
and
Go on Loving

Sharon Ries

KINGSWAY PUBLICATIONS
EASTBOURNE

First published in the USA by
Harvest House Publishers, Eugene, Oregon 97402

First British edition 1990

Biblical quotations are from the
The Holy Bible, New International Version, © 1973, 1978, 1984
by The International Bible Society. Anglicisation © 1979, 1984
by Hodder & Stoughton Ltd.

Front cover photo: Zefa Picture Library

British Library Cataloguing in Publication Data

Ries, Sharon
   To Love and go on loving.
   1. Christian Church, Evangelism – Biographies
   I. Title
   269.2092

   ISBN 0-86065-864-3

Printed in Great Britain for
KINGSWAY PUBLICATIONS LTD
1 St Anne's Road, Eastbourne, E Sussex BN21 3UN by
Richard Clay Ltd, Bungay, Suffolk.
Reproduced from the original text by arrangement with
Harvest House Publishers

To Chile,
Colombia . . .
and to the Uttermost Parts of the Earth.

Contents

The Harbor Lights

1

It was a muggy, windless summer day—a miserable day for traveling. Despite the steamy weather, Valparaiso—Chile's main port—was bustling with activity. All morning, dock workers had been hard at work loading our ship with cargo. Cranes with big hooks effortlessly swung crates, barrels, and boxes skyward, then lowered them through a large square opening on the main deck. During our voyage, that same deck area would be used for sunbathing.

The gray concrete shipyard with its drab, tin-roofed warehouses was brightened by throngs of people dressed in colorful clothing. My sister, Shirley, and I quietly studied the scene from the ship's deck, exchanging whispered comments about the rich women who promenaded below us, their fine jewelry gleaming in the sunlight. We pretended we were rich, too. This wasn't especially difficult because Mother always dressed us elegantly. That day we wore cheerful yellow eyelet dresses made for us by our family seamstress in Santiago.

Mother was a happily married, tall, green-eyed blonde who always looked beautiful and behaved likewise.

Shirley and I giggled, watching various sailors and male passengers staring at her. We were proud to be her daughters.

Our ship was called *La Reina del Mar*, one of the many British ocean liners that sailed the waterways of the world. In the early 1960s, this particular liner made its way through the Panama Canal between England and Chile, stopping at major ports along the Caribbean Sea and the Pacific Ocean.

The liner was an extravagant mini-city, complete with dress shops, hair salons, and a glittering ballroom. Shirley and I explored every corner, feeling as if we were in a fantasy world. This environment was dramatically different from the simple, unpretentious missionary life we normally led.

On the passenger list were names of the rich and famous as well as the working class. Most of the wealthy were in the midst of extensive, worldwide journeys. They occupied the upper part of the liner, enjoying the most opulent quarters. Passengers going to specific destinations, such as tourists and international commuters like us, traveled second class. We were lodged in the middle section of the liner with only a few less comforts. Third class was located in the lowest sections of the ship. Students, military personnel, and passengers on the most limited budgets traveled there.

Mother said second class was a good place for us, but I felt differently. First class attracted me with its sparkling pool, glamorous dining area, and fine clothing. Shirley and I agreed to spend most of our time there.

As we continued to investigate our new surroundings, a woman with an English accent interrupted us. "Come to dinner, girls," she instructed, guiding us through long hallways, up the stairs, and into a very formal dining area. The lavish red carpet and spotless white tablecloths were a little intimidating. Long-stemmed red roses formed the centerpieces on tables which were finely arrayed with silver and crystal. "You will sit here with the children and your parents will dine later on this evening," our guide primly explained.

Ever the impulsive one, I nudged my sister. "I don't like this. Why can't we sit with Mother?"

"It's probably because you're only 13 and look so young," responded Shirley, who had just turned 15. It was evident that she had matured a lot faster than I.

Fortunately, Mother quickly came to our rescue. "You two got captured by the first-class child attendant," she smiled. "But don't worry, in second class, we all eat together."

Mother hurriedly led the way back through the hallways, down the stairs, and onto the main deck. "Our friends are on the docks waiting to see us off. Daddy is looking for you, too," she spoke a little breathlessly. It would be a few months before our father would catch up with us in the United States. He planned to stay behind in order to turn our ministry over to new missionaries.

I didn't want to be reminded of the realities this trip represented. For me it was a nightmare, and I wanted to wake up soon. My parents had been missionaries in Chile since I was just four years old. Although I had spent my first four years in Colombia, Chile was all I knew. Nevertheless, Mother and Daddy had decided to take us to the United States to learn the English language and to receive an American education. But the length of our stay was unclear, and my heart was breaking. Chile was home—the home of my friends, the mission, my neighborhood . . . and the boy I loved.

Besides, why couldn't Daddy come with us? It never seemed possible for him to travel with us because of the overwhelming amount of work he always had to do. I yearned to see him have fun and relax, to watch him spend time with Mother. Would we ever have time to talk? If we did, would I be really open and frank with him—open enough to pour out my hurts about leaving Chile? Surely he was sorry about leaving too.

Deep inside, however, I knew that I would never say a word. Kids in Chile didn't question their parents. They just obeyed and suffered silently.

I would miss Daddy. I continuously missed him because he spent so little time with us. His work involved teaching Bible school every night as well as overseeing all our denomination's Chilean churches. His responsibilities required a lot of traveling. But Daddy loved people, especially the poor, lonely, and rejected. His life was devoted to them.

Although the pressures of life sometimes triggered an explosive temper, Daddy had a fun-loving, jovial character overall. Daddy always brought us wonderful gifts from his journeys. It was fun to wait for his return, trying to guess what he would bring us next. He would provide items like gum, candy bars, and jars of peanut butter. We made the peanut butter last for months. Shirley would spread it on thin so it would last longer. I hated it thin, so I would spread it on thick and eat one slice of bread to every two of hers. One time he had made a trip to the United States and brought us some pure nylon dresses. I lost an entire sleeve of one to a very hot iron. Daddy hid the gum and candy in a trunk with three locks which he kept in a little storage room in our house. The room also had two padlocks on its door. Chileans were especially attracted to our American cargo. Daddy would open the locks every so often and let us pick out a stick of gum and a candy bar.

These memories were scrambled in my mind as we finally found ourselves on the overcrowded deck. "There you are, girls!" Dad exclaimed, handsomely dressed in a neatly pressed beige suit.

He took us both in his arms and kissed us. We both automatically rubbed our lips, because his pencil-thin, red mustache left a tingling sensation. "Now remember, don't wear your new watches when you get off at the ports. Otherwise you might have them stolen."

I noticed tears gathering in his green eyes, although he tried to hide them. I couldn't cry even though I wanted to. Everything hurt too badly. My heart beat fast. My throat was dry.

Daddy was the last to get off the ship, just before the stairs were removed. I waved goodbye to our Chilean friends, who disappeared into the background as my eyes focused on Daddy. All too soon the distance erased him and the whole traumatic scene from my sight.

I wanted to run, but there was nowhere to go except down to our living quarters. There I could be alone. I climbed onto the bunk with a porthole facing the docks. I watched, my young heart aching, as the land I loved slipped away. I couldn't hold on no matter how hard I tried.

Memories carried me back to another farewell. I remembered being just four years old, leaving the United States. As I'd clung to one end of some crepe paper streamers, our relatives on the docks had grasped the other end. At last the distance had forced the colorful streamers to break. This time I made a vow. "Distance will never break my ties with you," I spoke softly into the porthole. Realizing that I was talking to myself, I directed my conversation toward God.

I had always talked to God, but never with such intensity as now. "God, do You know what I am feeling? Do you care that I am being stripped away from the beautiful country I dearly love?" He didn't answer. I hoped He had heard, even though He couldn't possibly be concerned with every heartache of every single person in the whole world.

But then, He is God, I thought. Maybe He does answer every single request. Maybe He does give each person everything he longs for. "Please, God, let me come back home soon," I earnestly pleaded with Him.

I couldn't imagine life in another country. Would I be greeted at dawn by a sight as majestic as the snowcapped Andes Mountains? Would the beaches have tide pools, swarming with shellfish, reflecting beautiful sunsets? Would the cities pulsate with life? Would there be a place where the kids meet while the hand-organ man plays and his little monkey sways for a peso or two? Would the streets be lined with vendors displaying their snacks from ship-shaped carts, smoke curling out of their smoke stacks? Would there be vast sand dunes to roll on and lush campsites, complete with waterfalls?

I would sorely miss the sprawling mission house with its magnificent garden, and the succulent snacks we enjoyed from its trees. And as for my Monopoly partners, the Bible school students, and the cook—when would I see them again? I couldn't imagine life without Chile. And even less could I imagine living without Fernando.

Fernando Leighton and I had met when I was 12. Although he had recently moved, he remained a part of a very special neighborhood gang from the double deadend street where we lived. We gathered together every evening beside a white wrought-iron fence to share good times and laughter.

Sometimes we all played hide-and-seek and some of us would disappear between the houses to hold hands and kiss. Panchy, a little red-haired, freckle-nosed friend, was invariably selected to count. "98 . . . 99 . . . 100!" she would yell, and then proceed to find us. It wasn't long before she tired of our romantic little game and went home to bed.

Now the events of the night before lingered sadly in my thoughts. I had walked with Fernando to the bus stop, unable to think of anything to say to him. We hadn't spoken a word—just held hands and stared at each other. Young as we were, I always knew what Fernando was thinking by the look in his eyes.

There were so many things I wished I had said. Yet somehow, the night before, it had taken all the courage I had just to utter one question. "Do you have a picture I can take with me to remember you by?" Fernando had reached into his pocket and had given me his I.D. picture. "I have more than that to remember you by," he said quietly.

He then said goodbye with a soft, gentle kiss. And now he was gone.

I closed my eyes and concentrated on him—his hazel eyes, his fair skin, his wavy, black hair. I never wanted to forget his face. For me, Fernando was the epitome of beauty and genuine gentleness. There was a sadness in his countenance that I never understood or asked about. No matter—he only had eyes for me and I knew it. And someday I would come back to him.

My thoughts faded as I realized that the land was now almost completely out of sight. Some words from a popular melody played softly in my hurting heart:

> I saw the harbor lights
> They only told me we were parting,
> The same old harbor lights
> That once brought you to me....

The land was gone. Just a couple of faraway lights twinkled somewhere near the now-darkened horizon. I felt lost at sea. I had no home, no friends, no Chile—only emptiness and pain. One unbearable thought sent rippling chills along my spine: "What if I can never come back?"

Looking for a City

2

"Wake up!" The airline stewardess gently shook my arm. "We're coming into Los Angeles!" I'd slept all the way from Panama City, where we had transferred from our ship to an airplane. Past experience had taught me that flying had a bad effect on my stomach, so I had decided to sleep the hours away.

The aerial view of southern California's nightlife was the most incredible sight I could have possibly imagined. It looked as if God had spilled a handful of luminous glitter over the land. Rain had washed the air clean, and as the plane slowly dropped in altitude, I could see streetlights mirrored on the wet pavements.

Los Angeles throbbed with activity. Broad highway arteries, larger than any I had ever seen, pumped thousands of tiny vehicles in and out of the heart of the city. I felt a surprising exhilaration that interrupted the sorrow I had experienced since leaving Chile two weeks earlier.

"I'll enjoy myself while I'm here," I decided, "and I'll learn to speak English." After all, didn't most of my friends dream of coming to the United States? "Then, when my visit is over, I'll go home." This final thought lingered until it was interrupted by the sound of our plane's wheels hitting the runway.

We passed through customs and eventually emerged into the airport reception area. Several long and lanky relatives, some with vaguely familiar faces, greeted us with tears of joy and "welcome home!" phrases I scarcely understood.

"Chile's food must have made the girls short," I heard mother laugh. But height wasn't the only thing that set us apart. Shirley and I could immediately see that, having lived all our lives in South America, we were thoroughly foreign, not only in language but in culture.

During the next few hectic days, mother wasted no time moving us into a tiny one-bedroom, one-bath guest house behind the residence of my grandpa, Reverend Lee Roy M. Kopp. We were amazed to watch mother transform that little, abandoned place into a sunny, yellow dollhouse which we called "home" for the next 12 months.

"When Daddy comes from Chile, we'll get our own place," she assured us. "Then you'll have a bedroom of your own."

Soon Christmas was just around the corner. Grandma Kopp enthusiastically introduced Shirley and me to her much-too-small-for-baking kitchen. "Why I've had my cookie cutters since I was a young woman."

"They look like it too!" Shirley giggled.

"And those big jars of rainbow-colored sugar are from Knott's Berry Farm!" She wanted us to enjoy her kitchen, and we did. We had never seen anything like it.

Every year she made a basket of homemade cookies and candies for each of her six children and their families. The 11 grandchildren would each receive a real silver dollar wrapped in bright-colored cellophane, trimmed with a neatly curled ribbon. Shirley and I were thrilled to help Grandma make the 1001 cookies for her yearly presentation. "Now, each cookie must be individually cut, baked, and decorated," she instructed, demonstrating her technique on a gingerbread man. "Then we'll distribute them into the six baskets."

I was deeply impressed by Grandma's ability to love each individual in the family equally. She'd barely become acquainted with Shirley and me, and yet we were just as close to her heart as the other grandchildren she knew so well.

Christmas arrived, and with it came our relatives. At that time, everyone we met was from Mother's family. My father's mother lived in South Sioux City, Nebraska, and the rest of his family was scattered in different cities throughout the United States. We later visited with them.

Mother had given us some family background before we left Chile. "A lot of my relations are pastors, Bible teachers, and musicians," she had explained. Somehow, my preconceived notion of this "priesthood family" had been of drab men, and of women wearing long black skirts, no makeup, and having tightly rolled buns on the back of their heads. What a relief it was to discover that they were not at all the way I had pictured them!

As a matter of fact, Shirley and I were amazed by the sight of our aunts, uncles, and cousins. One by one they arrived, wearing a broad variety of clothing which included everything from the ultraconservative to the most stylish, multi-colored fashion items.

"I like them," I thought to myself, feeling proud to be part of such a handsome group of men and women.

That first North American Christmas brought an all-new meaning to the season. It was more than being in a Chilean Christmas play, forgetting my lines, with Daddy taking far too many pictures. It was more than sharing Christmas dinner with friends and a few misplaced, lonely people who we invited to our home on Christmas Eve. It was more than receiving a beautiful homemade doll, while being reminded by my parents to give last year's doll away to a child who didn't have one.

That Christmas taught me a new dimension in giving. I listened, transfixed, as Grandpa Kopp shared his missionary journeys to the Holy Land, practicing his Hebrew on us. Meanwhile Uncle Paul described in great detail his own journeys to Israel, and the miracles that God had done there. I noticed how his wife, my Aunt Betty, lovingly admired him. I heard my cousin Janet calling me "my cuz," which gave me a warm sense of belonging. Cousin Connie said, "I love you." Up until then, that tender phrase had only been expressed to me by my parents.

After the very last piece of pumpkin pie had been devoured, Grandma called us together, and her fingers began to skillfully move across the piano keys. "Okay, everybody. Let's all gather around the piano and thank God for His wonderful love!"

Singing with that family was like being in a church choir. We all knew our parts. Even though Shirley and I didn't recognize all the songs, we harmonized anyway.

Finally, to everyone's delight, Grandma sang one of her own melodies. She had written it to express the deepest longing of her heart—being with Jesus in His heavenly city. It reflected the hopes and dreams of nearly everyone there. Young and old alike, these people knew Jesus Christ in a personal, intimate way. They sincerely looked forward to spending eternity with Him.

Tears ran down Grandma Kopp's cheeks as she sang with all her might:

> Some Golden Daybreak, Some happy day!
> Some Golden Daybreak, We shall see Christ!
> Break through the heavens, With power
>   and glory!
> Some Golden Daybreak . . .

Glancing around the room, I noticed that everyone was communicating some form of tenderness toward the person next to him. Some were holding hands, others stood arm in arm. Tears were running down our cheeks. Then unexpectedly, nostalgia waylaid my thoughts.

Suddenly my own longings caused me to envision a different kind of "golden daybreak." Much as I appreciated the spiritual yearnings of my relatives, heaven was not a priority for me at that time. Some golden daybreak would find me returning to the earthly city I longed for—Santiago, Chile.

I imagined myself gracefully disembarking from a white ocean liner wearing a slim, white suit. My long, red hair was flowing in the wind, burnished by the sun's rays. The dock was swarming with people, but one person stood out above them all: Fernando. He was taller, more handsome, and had grown remarkably mature.

Our eyes locked, and I fell into his arms.

I loved Christmas. I had greatly enjoyed my new fellowship with our long-separated family. But nothing brought me more joy than the thought of loving and being loved. It was my favorite dream.

No promise of some faraway heaven was about to take it away from me.

A
Shooting Star

3

After my arrival in America, I received and answered dozens of letters from Fernando. In time I became weary of our relationship, realizing that distance would never permit it to mature.

Correspondence during the three years of our separation revealed dramatic changes in our lives. Fernando was becoming an extremely literate and productive young man. Although in some ways our friendship had richly deepened, I was saddened by the fact that life was taking us in different directions. Inevitable changes develop during long separations, but along with those, Fernando had acquired some beliefs at the university that diametrically opposed mine. There was no end to the agony of our being apart, and I found my interest in writing letters slowly diminishing. Regretfully, I tucked Fernando's warm memory away in my heart.

By then I was 16 years old, beginning my junior year in high school. The first time I noticed Raul, it was fall—a season that I loved. The school's lawns were scattered with an infinite variety of the Creator's individually designed leaves. As I gazed out the classroom window at this delightful scene, the lunch bell rang.

I dashed out of class and rushed across campus, hoping to beat most of the student body to the front of the lunch line. All at once I noticed someone carelessly approaching me in a loose-fitting white T-shirt and a pair of very faded blue jeans. I slowed down, hoping to get a better look.

Yes—just as I thought, he was gorgeously built, handsomely designed, and wonderfully beautiful. True, he was young, and I liked older guys. But his greenish-brown eyes; his tanned, fine-featured face; and his black, wavy hair made him very acceptable. My first impression was that he summed up the ultimate dashing Spanish conqueror, and at that moment I definitely wanted to be conquered. Fortunately we made immediate eye contact.

"Hi ya," he said, eyeing me from head to toe.

"Hi," I answered breathlessly.

It seemed like a good beginning. But much to my dismay, our future encounters remained identical to our first. At this pace, I would never be conquered! Well, that was just fine. I didn't have time to worry about him because, after all, he seemed a bit immature. Besides, I had plenty of other interests to keep me busy.

By now our family had moved to a comfortable home. Daddy had a good job and was pursuing some opportunities for higher education. Our new lives in the United States required continuous adjustment, and carried responsibilities I had never known before.

Some of my spare time was spent designing and sewing clothes for Mother, Shirley, and me. In Chile, it was a job either Mother or our seamstress had always done. I was glad to have inherited it, because I loved fashion. I even sewed for other people, earning extra money in order to keep my closet jammed with all the latest fads.

Going to church with the family also absorbed a lot of my time. Participation in plays, musicals, and social events was a source of genuine pleasure for me. I especially admired our pastor, Carl Green. This man loved young people. He said caring, important things that caused me to make meaningful decisions that would impact my life forever.

One Sunday, as tears rolled down his cheeks, he said, "God has a special plan for each one of you young people. To discover that plan, you must get to know Him. . . . You must talk to Him, read His words, meditate upon them, and then do what He says. If you give your life entirely to Jesus, He will guide you and you will find life, for He is the life."

And so I turned my life over to Him—again and again and again. "God, I want to know You," I would plead. "Who are You? What do You want from me? How can I know Your will? God, please forgive my sins. Forgive the things I do that are not pleasing to You, and make me the way You want me to be."

I made spiritual promises to myself that I could not possibly keep. My hectic life prevented me from really concentrating on God's Word. I didn't have much time to meditate or to obey. But I did talk to Him about my problems every night.

I was very involved in high school. Since the first day that I arrived onto an American school campus, I was accepted by my peers. However I harbored fears of not fitting in, and in some areas could not relate at all to the "American way." After spending a couple of weeks hiding in the school halls during lunchtime with my sister, I was invited to join a group of girls who were involved in all kinds of school activities. Leadership had always been a natural aspect of my life, so by the time I became a junior, I had been involved in the Pep Club, German Club, Drill Team, Student Class Council, and several other activities. When I became a senior I was elected as one of the Drill Team heads and as Director of Finance for the Associated Student Body.

Each year the athletes at our school hosted an all-sports dance for which they chose a court of princesses. I had always shied away from these very "popular" fellows. Although I seldom missed a sports event and cheered fanatically for the participants, unlike the boys I had been raised around, they seemed too aggressive and forward for me. However, my junior year I was chosen by the tennis team, which at the time was made up of the studious guys on campus. Some of them were my classmates, hence I was deeply honored to represent them.

It was spring, and my relationship with Raul still had not grown past the "Hi ya, you look great" stage. Since the princesses were responsible for getting their own escorts, I saw this as a great opportunity to invite Raul to the dance. This was a particularly radical step for me, because asking a boy to go out was impermissible in my traditional Chilean upbringing.

I stayed up half the night before I asked him, finishing the new dress I planned to wear the next day. I got up extra early so I could brush my freshly-washed, long hair at least 100 times. Mascara and eyeliner went on neater and thicker than ever. Having taken great care with every possible detail of my appearance, I made my way to school and waited by Raul's locker until he came by.

"Hi, Raul."

"Hi, how are you doing, Sharon?"

"Can I talk to you?" I asked shyly.

"Sure." A mischievous smile played around his lips, and he eyed me intensely.

"Well, I've been chosen to be Tennis Princess at the All-Sports Dance. I was wondering if you could escort me." I went on to explain why I wasn't inviting my regular boyfriend. "Mike is out of school, so he can't go with me."

"Sure," he answered coolly.

Since my disillusionment with Fernando, I had been dating Mike. He was both fun and good-looking. I'd been crazy about him until I met Raul. Mike regularly attended church with me, but neither of us ever had really matured spiritually.

Although I enjoyed and respected Mike, I couldn't get Raul off my mind. I had heard somewhere that Raul admired Mike's "street fighting" techniques. Apparently they were very similar to his. Eventually the night of the All-Sports Dance arrived. I zipped myself into the white organdy dress I had designed. It was lined and trimmed in yellow taffeta, and was gorgeous enough to hold its own among the array of dresses that would grace the princesses' court. After stacking my hair on top of my head in a cascade of curls, I waited nervously for Raul.

"So who's Raul?" asked Mother, admiring me in my finished dress project.

"Just a friend from school," I responded.

"Is he a Christian?"

"I don't know, Mother. He's just my escort tonight. I don't plan on marrying him."

"Boys" was the only topic I avoided discussing with my parents. Daddy's repeated counsel was continuously hammered into our minds. "Get an education, follow a career, and don't think about boys till you're 26. About that time God will bring you together with the man of His choice, just like He did with your Mother and me."

Mother's concern was that we date boys who loved God. "If he loves Jesus, he will want to do His will. And he will always want to love you, too."

It always sounded so simple when they were saying it, but in reality their instructions created great conflict within me. I enjoyed dating much more than running around with a bunch of silly girls. But most of all, I craved being cared for, and thrived on conversation and companionship. As for waiting for that elusive "Christian boy," I was already 17 years old, had spent all my life in church, and had never yet come across one that appealed to me.

My compromise, therefore, would be to take my boyfriends to church. There I would see that they were introduced to God, and the "Christian boy" problem would be solved for all of us.

"Well, you look beautiful," Mother smiled. "I have to keep an eye out for my girl, you know."

"Thanks, Mom. I love you."

The doorbell rang. I introduced a very well-behaved Raul to my parents, and we left. The hours that followed soon became one of the most fun-filled nights of my life. We laughed, we danced, but mostly we simply looked at each other. I couldn't think of anything to say. What I was feeling seemed too deep to discuss on a first date. I stored the thoughts away in my heart along with the rest of my treasured memories.

Raul took me home without even a hint about seeing me again. Our relationship soon slowed back down to its normal "hi ya" pace. But my desire to be with him grew steadily, and continued into my senior year.

Throughout that year, the main theme around campus was the Vietnam war. Which senior boys would get drafted? Some would escape by pursuing education, others would have to go, and many would probably volunteer. No one would admit to being afraid. Personally, I couldn't imagine anyone going to war when education was such an easy out.

I started making my own plans for the future. I loved attending school, and determined that I would get a good education. I wanted to major in Social Science and minor in Spanish. This would be the logical course to prepare me for my return to Chile.

At our school, homecoming was the biggest event of the year. Senior princesses were chosen by the entire student body and were honored during halftime at a hard-hitting football game. Being the over-involved senior that I was made me one of the eligible candidates. My classmates voted for me, and once again I found myself needing an escort to a very important dance.

As before, Raul accepted my invitation. What a thrill it would be to spend one of the year's memorable events with him. As far as I was concerned, he was the most fabulous, fun-loving guy in all the world.

Two days before the event, he telephoned.

"Hello, Sharon. This is Raul."

"Hi, Raul! Are you ready for Friday night?"

"Yeah. Well, that's what I called about. I'm really sorry, Sharon, but I won't be able to take you. See, I got in a little fight last weekend at a party and now the school won't let me go to homecoming."

"Just because of a little rumble?" I was devastated.

"Well, you know how they are."

Heartsick, I hung up the phone. Everything had gone wrong. Not only had I lost my long-awaited date with Raul, but my reproduction of one of Jacqueline Kennedy's ball gowns had turned out to be a total flop. Surrounded by rumpled white satin and my sewing gear, I sat on the floor and wept. I felt like Cinderella, except I would never make it to the ball.

"Oh God," I prayed, "why do my plans always fall apart? Why can't I ever have the boy I want?" I always talked to God more when things went wrong.

Mother invariably brought order to my chaos. She calmly walked into my room, picked up "Jackie's" dress, examined it thoughtfully, then laid it down without comment. She proceeded to rummage around in my overstuffed closet and triumphantly pulled out a beautiful coral chiffon dress I had worn in my cousin Janet's wedding. She ripped the veil off the pearl-beaded headpiece and quietly said, "This is what a princess should wear!"

A male friend escorted me during the halftime ceremony. Although I was deeply honored to participate in the gala event, I fought an overwhelming sense of disappointment. One very important missing person could have made that night a dream-come-true.

One of Mother's many proverbs struggled to penetrate my preoccupied mind. I could almost hear her voice saying, "Jesus is the only Prince you'll ever need." But at that moment, someone else was on my mind.

After the dance began, led by the princesses and their escorts, my friend had to leave. I was left alone in my coral dress, pearl-beaded crown and all. I decided to be depressed, and proceeded to do so.

Barely a moment had passed when, all of a sudden, I noticed some mischievous eyes watching me behind the stage curtain. I ran backstage, and there was Raul. He had sneaked in. His lawlessness scared me, but not enough to make me run away.

"How's my princess doing tonight?" he grinned.

"Miserable without you!" The words found their way out of my mouth before I had time to catch them.

"How 'bout a dance?" he asked, impulsively taking me into his arms. We laughed, acted crazy, and gazed into each other's eyes till the clock struck 12.

After homecoming, our relationship slowly began to grow and continued to do so until graduation. I never greeted Raul that he didn't tell me how beautiful I looked, and how much he wanted to date me. It would have seemed obvious that he was in love with me, but for some reason he never asked me out. I silently hoped, and once again, I waited.

"And I'll wait forever," I determined in my heart.

Graduation was near. Some of my friends were investing in fabulous dresses at expensive stores. This time I designed mine early so it wouldn't end up in the ragbag. It was a total-white-eyelet success.

Everybody wanted a special date for graduation evening, and I was no exception. I knew very well whom I wanted to be with, but this time it wasn't my place to ask. I didn't.

After receiving the congratulations of family, friends, and loved ones, the senior class exuberantly crowded into several buses. They would take us to Long Beach Harbor where we would embark on an all-night cruise to Catalina Island. Our destination was one last occasion of shared laughter, friendship, and fun.

I squeezed into a seat at the front of the bus. It wasn't long before I was overwhelmed by an invasion of fearful thoughts. Emotionally, I was a mess. Fernando was a dream that had refused to come true. Mike was no more than a sweet memory. And Raul? He was like a mirage that would never become reality. There I sat, alone again.

Our commencement ceremony had caused other questions to crowd my mind as well. Would I be able to achieve the high goals I had set for myself? College seemed like such a complicated prospect. Various ambitions would soon scatter my classmates to the four corners of the world. Would I ever see them again? What would take the place of cheering at football games? Of cruising local burger hangouts in a '57 Chevy stuffed with screaming, giggling girls? Of staying after school for student council meetings?

Was there life after high school?

Would I ever get to go back to Chile?

When we got off the buses, we scrambled for the ship like a bunch of lifelong prisoners being set free. I was herded right through the door and immediately found myself on the wide dance floor. Only a second could have passed before my eyes focused on Raul's, all the way across the room. This time something different gleamed in their brown-green depths. They seemed to say that the long-awaited conquest of my heart was about to begin.

It did. We spent the night walking around the deck, holding hands, staring at each other. Words were unnecessary. Memories of Chile, Fernando, and Mike stood as still as the constellations on a moonless night. A shooting star had flashed across the sky, interrupting my life. I was destined to follow it.

That night, Raul and I set sail into a new tomorrow. My head resting on his shoulder, I couldn't quite understand my emotions. I could only feel that the sea was calm, and all was well.

What would tomorrow bring?

Navigating On My Own

4

A warm, breezy June afternoon found Raul and me sitting on my front porch. I wasn't allowed to entertain boys in the house when no one else was home, so we were enjoying each other's company along with the outdoor scenery. Daddy had surrounded our house with a lush carpet of grass, bordering it with a variety of seasonal flowers and tree roses.

Under my window he had planted a white camellia just for me.

"You've enlisted in the Marine Corps?" Horrified, I repeated Raul's statement to be sure I'd understood.

"Don't worry, Sharon. . . . I'll write to you every day!" He tried to pacify me by kissing my cheek repeatedly.

I'll write to you. . . . A familiar pain threatened. I remembered the many letters Fernando and I had exchanged. Some of their memorized lines slowly tiptoed across my mind.

"But you don't understand . . ." I wanted to explain, but couldn't.

"Don't worry . . . everything is going to be just fine," Raul interrupted.

"So where will you go?" I asked.

"To boot camp in San Diego for eight weeks, and then . . . somewhere in the world!" he continued, kissing me between words.

His exhilaration bothered me. The fact that we would be separated didn't seem to concern him in the least. And besides, what if he ended up in Vietnam? What if he got killed? Loneliness once more stood at the door of my life trying to push itself inside. But Raul's persistent teasing, laughter, and intermittent kisses distracted my thoughts. All was well—for the moment.

He left for boot camp vowing that I would hear from him and, to my surprise, I did. In every letter he begged me to wait for him, and he continuously promised that he would "change." Waiting had become a painful way of life for me. But I couldn't understand why he needed to change. I loved him just the way he was . . . fun, visionary, and most of all, affectionate. His zest for life sparkled like a fountain, and I wanted to splash in it!

Raul had enlisted for a four-year tour of duty with the Marines, so I proceeded with my intentions to get an education and to fulfill some of my dreams. My plans invariably included my sister. Shirley and I had always been best friends. It's unbelievable but, as far back as I can remember, the number of fights we've had can be counted on one hand.

I wanted to work full-time during the day and go to night school. Shirley felt that it made perfect sense for me to get a job at the electronics factory where she worked. She made a strong case for my taking a job there.

"You'll make good money. And you can study while you work, because the job doesn't require you to use your brain. Besides, we can ride to work together."

Shirley and I never imagined that we would be apart. At night, after the lights were out, we planned our entire lives together as we always had. After our nightly bedtime chats with Mother, like typical Chileans we stayed

up late and talked, often past midnight. Shirley was the
one with all the ideas.

"First, we'll go to Europe. We'll visit Paris, Rome,
Venice, London, and Madrid. Then we'll go back to
Chile and you can see Fernando!"

"What's it like in London?" I listened, spellbound,
while she described the faraway places she loved so
much to envision.

Shirley seemed to know everything. She read to me
while I sewed for her. She devoured travel books and
magazines, studied maps, and memorized tour pam-
phlets. She calculated that we could go to Europe on five
dollars per day. "And that includes lodging, food, and
transportation!"

We prayed for God's blessing on our decisions and
went to sleep dreaming of adventures.

Meanwhile, the environment of my full-time factory
job brought society's hopelessness into full view. People
at work seemed to be going nowhere. Their personal
goals amounted to getting a raise and taking weekends
off. Foolish, dirty talk dominated almost every conversation. The whole scene posed a grave threat to either
intellectual or spiritual growth.

Shirley and I contented ourselves with plans for better
tomorrows. She would become an international airline
stewardess, satisfying her wanderlust. I, too, expected
to do something daring and unique.

At the end of eight weeks, Raul's boot camp was over
and I received a phone call from his mother. "Sharon?
This is Josie. Raul called and he wants us to take you with
us to his graduation from basic training."

"Thanks for asking," I answered respectfully, "but
I'm already planning to go with a girlfriend." A new
worry entered my heart: Would his parents, brother, and
sisters like me?

The day came. A brilliant blue sky stretched all the

way from the Los Angeles suburbs to San Diego. When I arrived there, I met a delightful family.

First, petite Josie ran over to meet us. My Latin American upbringing enabled me to recognize the pure Spanish blood that ran thick in her veins. She was a handsome, fine-featured lady. Papi, Raul's dad, reflected the well-built sturdiness of his half-German, half-Mexican breeding. Josie was loud and bubbly; Papi was amusing, but more reserved.

Raul had a younger brother, Xavier. He also had two sisters, Sonia, a 12-year-old beauty, and little Chrissy, with whom I fell in love at first sight.

The Ries family made it quite clear that they were extremely pleased with Raul's choice of a girlfriend. Papi seemed especially impressed at my ability to rattle off Spanish fluently. He tested me with countless questions and smiled approvingly at my answers.

Our chatter was stilled as we walked across the Marine base together, and our attention was drawn from each other and toward hundreds of perfectly regimented, meticulously uniformed Marines. They marched up and down the spotless parade grounds chanting their marching cadences.

Once Raul came on the scene, I saw no one but him. I was amazed by his appearance. A little bit of strenuous exercise could certainly make an already beautiful human specimen even more spectacular! It also pleased me to learn that this young man was not only fascinating to look at, but a top achiever. He graduated with high honors. The family was proud. He was perfect. I silently hoped that he was mine.

"Yes, I will wait for him," I resolved. What else could I do? I felt somehow as if I had found a missing puzzle piece that completed the picture of my life. I welcomed him into my world, even though I knew it would mean being alone.

That September, Raul received his infantry training at
Camp Pendleton near San Diego. After a couple of letters, he stopped writing. I couldn't believe how obsessed
with him I had become. Once more I found myself waiting endlessly for the mailman to appear.

Thinking of Raul made my schoolwork far more difficult. How could I have let this happen to me again? The
days became endless. An empty feeling haunted me.

Around the first of December, on an unusually chilly
day, I unexpectedly met Raul face-to-face at a neighborhood market.

He looked startled. "Hi, Sharon. How are you doing?"

"What are you doing home?" My voice must have
given evidence of my dismay.

"Oh, I've been on leave. Tomorrow I'm being shipped
out to Vietnam."

I wanted to ask him why he hadn't written or called,
but I couldn't. I didn't want to hear him say it was over.
But he anticipated my question. And he answered it with
a lie.

"Sorry I haven't been in touch, Sharon. They wouldn't
let us write to anybody. And since I've been home, I've
been too busy getting ready to leave." Later I learned that
he'd been home nearly a month and had spent the whole
time with his school buddies.

"Well, I gotta go. It was nice seeing you." I walked
toward my car, shivering and humiliated.

Raul followed me out, "Sharon . . . I'm sorry. I mean it.
I really do want you to be my only girl—honest. Do you
think there's any possibility? Do you think a guy like me
can have a girl like you?"

Right then I knew, with all my heart, that this was my
cue to run away from him—to run with all of my
strength. Whatever love I felt for him was of a different
dimension than any I had known before, but I sensed
danger. My thoughts were scrambled. Past experience
warned me to stop the relationship. My upbringing

screamed at me to turn and go. Then, as usual, my will
yielded. Raul had convinced me to try again.

From that decision onward, I drifted with a tide of
events that cost me unimaginable sorrow.

As I drove home, Mother's soft, instructive voice rose
above my confused thoughts: "A relationship with a
person whose life is not centered on God can only bring
heartache."

I was well-acquainted with the misery caused by separation, but the pain I was feeling now was different.
Raul's silence, his lies, and then his unexplainable desire
for me to be his girl generated distrust and insecurities I
had never dealt with before. I rationalized that all my
relationships had been hurtful in one way or another.
And I still hadn't located that ideal Christian boyfriend.

When Raul left for Vietnam, he didn't want me to see
him off. But before he left, he called. There was an
unusual tone of desperation in his voice, although he
attempted to sound jovial as ever.

"Promise you'll write?" he asked repeatedly.

"I promise. I'm a master at it!" I assured him.

"Do you think we're going to make it?" He sounded
genuinely worried.

"I don't know Raul. We will if it's God's will."

"I love you, Sharon. Honest. I'm going to miss you."

"I'll miss you too," I answered, beginning to believe
him. As we said goodbye, tears drenched my face.

This time Raul kept his word. He wrote from the
U.S.S. *Gaffi*, his departure ship. He wrote from Da Nang,
his arrival city. He wrote from camp, from the bush,
from the U.S.S. *Sanctuary* after being wounded. He even
wrote from Japan.

As I read his letters, I sometimes wondered if he was
dead. I cried a lot, and studied his pictures under the
microscopes at work. Each new letter brought the assur-
ance of his ongoing life and hope for the future. By now
he was making lots of plans for us.

"Please wait for me. I'm coming home. I promise. When I do, will you marry me?"

I always responded that I couldn't marry him because he wasn't a Christian. But, besides that, I didn't fully trust him. I tried to tell him about the plans I had for my own life. "I want to serve God the way my parents always have. I want to discover the plans that God has for me. . . ."

Deep inside I firmly believed that one day I would be a missionary in some distant land.

"I *am* a Christian!" Raul would write, trying to convince me. "Didn't I go to church with you? Besides, I could never hurt you, because you're the only girl I've ever loved. I'm going to spend all my time with you—you'll see!"

His correspondence also revealed his need to be loved, and I wanted to love him. There was an emptiness in his nature that would be filled once he met Jesus. He was simple and uncomplicated, and in some ways childlike. But most of all he loved me, and I wanted to be loved by him. I was bent on waiting this one out.

One year passed. Daddy had been going to college classes with me at night. They were complex and exhausting, but his encouragement made it possible for me to persevere. My father never criticized me or said a single discouraging word. His enthusiasm convinced me to quit my boring job and to tackle an overloaded, daytime college schedule.

On the first day of school, I woke up before the alarm went off. I had wrestled all night with nightmares of lockers not opening, "F's" on my papers, vanished classrooms and, worst of all, being unable to understand wordy, philosophical lectures.

Undaunted, I jumped out of bed, threw on my prearranged-the-night-before outfit, and ran out the door, my schedule in one hand and a piece of toast in the other. I arrived an hour early so I could find my classes and the cafeteria, as well as places to study.

My interests had changed since high school. I was no longer fascinated by clothes or school events. I no longer strove to maintain friendships where I had nothing in common except school events. And because of Raul, boys were off-limits. My intellect, after 19 years, seemed to be awakening from a lifelong nap. A desire for academic achievement stirred within me. Meanwhile my spirit demanded answers to some serious questions. I wanted to settle, once and for all, my place in God's plan, and my reason for being alive.

Students and teachers alike disputed the existence of God. This was news to me. I was born believing in God, and couldn't recall a single day that I had not believed in Him. There were many matters beyond my understanding, and some of them puzzled me. But to disbelieve in God was out of the question.

One day a professor pridefully challenged, "I dare you to open your cluttered minds to discover the truth . . . the truth that there really is no God!"

I took his challenge without any reservations. I was convinced that if Jesus really was the only-begotten Son of the transcendent God, no man's lie could change that fact. I also concluded that if God was the Creator of all things as the Bible attests, then He would be revealed at the heart of any subject I studied. I went to my classes with an open mind, determined to learn all that I could.

After listening to more than a dozen professors, all with differing opinions concerning God and creation, I learned a very important truth: There might be as many opinions about God as there are people on this planet. But how could anyone determine who was telling the truth? Only God could speak for Himself!

As I faithfully sat in my classes day after day, I found that even scientists, knowledgeable as they were, had limited ability to understand anything fully. There were

appalling blanks in their theories, and many of their so-
called scientific facts were sadly lacking in scientific
evidence. It became clear to me that, just as the Scripture
says, all human knowledge is incomplete apart from
God. We only gain true wisdom as He reveals Himself
and His plans to us through creation, the Scriptures, and
through His Son, Jesus Christ.

One day my astronomy professor said, "Today we're
going to look into some of the marvelous discoveries
man has made during the last few decades." He went on
to describe facts, not visible to the naked eye, concerning
our universe. To my surprise, I had already read about
these things in my Bible. The biblical statements I had
read had been written with perfect accuracy thousands
of years prior to this class, before the telescope or the
microscope had even been invented.

I could see that neither students nor instructors were
necessarily interested in finding "truth." Instead, each
person was choosing to believe whatever would resolve
his own moral or intellectual dilemma without inter-
ference from a sovereign Lord. How hard they worked at
finding evidence to prove their ever-changing percep-
tions rather than to build solid theories on established
evidence. In every class I took, the Bible was absolutely
ignored. This was done in spite of the fact that it remains
the oldest and most reliable document ever written.

No one seemed impressed that, although the Bible
was written by 40 different authors over a period of 1600
years, it is unmatched in its uniformity and unchallenged
in its truth. Instead, hours of class time were spent
discussing the differing opinions of "thinkers" throughout history—men who went to their graves without ever
discovering the truth.

During those months I contemplated the universe
with its infinite wonders, radiant splendor, and perfect
order. Its complexity declared the existence of an omni-
scient, omnipotent Creator. "It's as if there had been a

master planner," admitted a professor one day as he explained how our entire solar system works together to produce the crop-growing season.

I learned that man, who is made in the image of his Creator and therefore is so like Him in his abilities to reason, discover, and create, often willfully chooses to remain ignorant of God. And this they knowingly do, even though evidence concerning His existence can be clearly seen in all that He has made. But, by His grace, I had not made this foolish choice. I began to feel wonderful! Not only had I always believed in God, but now I had begun to grasp the evidence concerning Him. The eternally existing God was my Maker!

In the meantime, I was doing well in school. My savings account was steadily growing, promising a summer of travel. And, to top it all, Raul came home unexpectedly.

High Tide

5

Raul limped toward me, tired and bruised. He wore battered battle fatigues and beat-up jungle boots. He moved stiffly, favoring the booby-trap wounds on his back and the shrapnel which remained embedded in his left leg. Dark circles ringed his eyes, bearing witness to his constant sleeplessness. He had had to remain ever-alert to an enemy attack. I gently caressed his face. He seemed so fragile...

"Sharon! Sharon, wake up, we're almost there!" Chrissy's enthusiastic young voice abruptly ended my favorite fantasy.

"You gonna give him a great big kiss?" Xavier was a tease. I laughed to cover my embarrassment.

"What'll you say to my brother?" Chrissy was possessive of Raul and was enjoying this spontaneous interrogation. "Are you going to marry him? What are you going to wear? I want to be in the wedding!"

"I don't know, Chrissy. What are you going to wear?" I laughed, trying to divert the questions back to her.

I certainly didn't have any answers for the Ries family's inquiries. The truth was, I had plenty of questions of my own.

We were all crowded into their Volkswagen van, making the eight-hour trip to Oakland Naval Hospital in northern California. Raul had called his parents early that morning, asking them to come to see him, and to bring me along. After 11 months of the most unbearable jungle warfare imaginable, he was extremely battle fatigued. He had been flown home from Vietnam two months before his expected return date. His family was overjoyed.

As for me, crammed into a vehicle with five people I didn't know very well, I was a nervous wreck. A chronic case of infatuation, ever-present uncertainty about the future, and the excitement of seeing Raul again had rendered me almost speechless. I stared out the window hoping to avoid any further conversations.

The fertile land which spans the distance between Los Angeles and San Francisco was ready for harvest, about to provide the abundant farm produce that makes California such a fruitful state. Fluffy clouds floated across the broad sky without a care in the world, obeying the course of nature as God designed them to do. Memories of another automobile journey carried me back to my tenth year.

During a visit to America, Daddy had packed Mother, Shirley and me, and our belongings into a new 1958 pink Rambler station wagon. We had barely enough room to sit. He had driven us mercilessly from one state to another in the midst of the most appallingly hot summer I had ever experienced.

Friends who had supported my parents on the mission field had invited us to visit their homes and churches, and to share our missionary adventures with them. Daddy was impressively skillful at bringing the people right into our world. His slide presentation boarded the viewers on an ocean liner and carried them to faraway lands where they encountered the joys and perils of our lives. The crowd laughed and cried and many men and women made new life-commitments to God.

Daddy had a passion for people which radiated from his entire being. "The harvest truly is great, but the laborers are few; pray ye therefore to the Lord of the harvest, that he would send forth laborers into his harvest." Daddy echoed the words of Jesus, and those words were burned into my own young heart.

"I'll go! I'll go! Send me!" I inwardly shouted. As far as I was concerned, the mission field was the only place to be.

Mother had heard the call in her heart to go "South of the Great River," as a young girl of 13. By the time she was 18, she was the director of the Interdenominational Youth Rallies in the greater Los Angeles area. Daddy, a bachelor of 26 just out of Bible college, visited one of these meetings on his way to the mission field. The moment he saw her walk in confidently "like an angel, dressed in white," he knew in his heart that God had brought her to him. They were married in eight months and on the mission field one year later.

Throughout our lives, Mother's love for God was expressed by her faithful support of Daddy in all that he did. During that trip, as always, Shirley and I made our own youthful contribution. We joined Mother, singing her favorite Spanish songs of adoration and thanksgiving to the Lord.

After church, pastors and their families would usually treat us to an all-American chicken, mashed potato, and gravy dinner. They would then kindly thank us and send us off, with a gift of money which enabled us to pay for our gas. Sometimes we stopped at drive-in restaurants along the highways. There we consumed our first hamburgers, Coke floats, and French fries. To our astonishment, they were served by teenage girls who roller-skated out to serve us through the windows of our car.

During the long, hot stretches of driving, Daddy taught us short history lessons and provided interesting facts about each state. Mother entertained us, singing both American folk songs and melodies of inspiration and faith. The setting sun prompted her to tell us one Bible story or another, lessons which buried priceless values in our hearts. She could never have imagined to what extent those informal teachings would guide me through times of doubt and darkness.

I missed Mother now. I needed Shirley to help me understand what was happening to me. I closed my eyes as I often did when I needed to sort things out.

"You're never alone," Mother had said many times.

My heart responded, "God is here, He's always here for me to talk to."

"What am I going to do?" I asked my Eternal Companion.

Raul had written that he wanted to get married once he got home. I wasn't ready for that at all. I still had two years of college to complete, and I knew that I could never marry until I returned to Chile.

I wonder what Fernando is doing? Painful recollections drifted into my thoughts. It had been such a long time since we had written to each other. I needed to return to Chile, to see about Fernando, before I could make any major decisions about the future.

I need time. Lots of time, I thought. *I need time to spend with Raul, to get to know him, to tell him about me, my plans, and my God. We'll go to church together,* I decided. *He'll get to know God and then it'll be alright with God for us to be together! I'll travel during the summer and finish college while he does his remaining two years in the Marines.*

It was a perfect plan. After all, I was only 19. Daddy always said 26 was a good age to get married. Satisfied with this decision, I concluded it would all work out.

A lively wind began to blow as we drove through San Francisco, clearing the city's pollution from the skies.

We had traveled all night and were hot, wrinkled, and uncombed. "Can't we go to the hotel first to get cleaned up?" My question was silently answered as I looked out the car window and saw the Oakland Naval Hospital.

Raul's dad gave us ten minutes to go to the ladies' restroom for toothbrushing and freshening up. There was no sense in arguing with him—we only had one hour to see Raul.

"Lance Corporal Ries will be out in a few minutes. Just have a seat out there," instructed a military police officer, pointing out a picnic table on the grass. As we waited, I looked around, surprised at the enormity of the naval hospital complex.

I tuned out Raul's chattering family and allowed my imagination to carry me away again. I relived my dream once more, picturing Raul in his weatherworn fatigues, emerging from his barracks, making his way straight for me, embracing me gently . . .

Just then I saw him. A chill started in my brain and crawled slowly down my spine. This was real life, and there was the Marine of my dreams, the one I had been waiting for. He was walking toward us wearing impeccable dress greens.

My fantasies had deceived me. He looked healthy and strong. As far as battle wounds were concerned, a very slight limp was the only noticeable change. Eleven months of warfare had matured him. He had become more handsome, very serious, and extremely masculine. The boyhood spark in his eyes had been replaced by a sharp, piercing look.

Something exploded inside me. All the long months of mixed emotions—fear and desire, mistrust and loyalty, longing and independence—combined into a feeling I had never known before. At that fateful moment, I didn't care whether Raul was a Christian or not. I didn't care what Raul was really like inside. I simply liked the Raul I saw, and I wanted him.

I sat quietly while his family hugged and kissed him. They must have asked him a hundred and one questions. Our eyes communicated frustration and the desire to be alone, but there was no time. There never was. The hour was gone with a kiss on the cheek and we were separated once again. How long would it be this time?

During the next six months, Raul was given a few weekend passes. The eight-hour trip from Oakland to Los Angeles and back left us with only a handful of hours to enjoy one another's company. This was made even more difficult by the fact that these were our first opportunities to be together in three years. Hours ticked by like seconds when I was with Raul. When he was gone, even minutes seemed to linger forever.

On the two Sundays he was home, he religiously accompanied me to church. He took communion and went to the altar to pray when the minister suggested it. Good Catholic that he was, he was trying to understand what my God was all about by going through the motions. Nevertheless, I was convinced that he was sincere in his religious gestures. Some day he would surely meet God for himself and would come to know Him personally.

After spending six months of mandatory therapy at Oakland Naval Hospital, Raul was transferred to Camp Pendleton, the Marine base two hours from our hometown where he had taken his infantry training. Not long after he relocated there, Easter rolled around. Raul asked some of his friends and his family to camp at a beach site near the marine base so he could spend a weekend with us.

"Sharon, why don't you and Raul go down early on Friday morning and reserve us a good campsite?" Josie suggested. "Papi and I will go over the border to Mexico, pick up some supplies, and meet you there Friday night."

Raul and I were ecstatic. At last we would be able to spend a few hours alone together before everyone arrived. We met as planned. An entire day with him

seemed like only a few minutes. No sunset had ever
been so lovely. While we waited, the twilight became
evening and the evening, dawn. Our kisses led to the
kind of passion that demands satisfaction.

Obviously, no one showed up—not even Raul's parents. We found out later that everyone had had a last-
minute change of plans.

We had met at the campsite on Good Friday. Now
Saturday's first brilliant rays broke across the horizon. I
had not slept all night. The beach was quiet and serene. I
wasn't.

The ocean's waves had pounded the shore all night,
washing away footprints and sand castles, leaving the
beach smooth and clean. How I wished the events that
had occurred there in the seaside darkness could have
been as easily washed out of my memory.

I had broken my vow with God.

All my life I had made promises to the Lord, believing
that in doing so I would somehow prevent myself from
disobeying Him. How could anyone break a promise to
God? The fact was, I had managed to do it more often
than I cared to recall. This time it was serious. I knew it
was.

"Why?" I asked myself. "Why couldn't I live up to
God's laws?"

While driving home, Raul seemed incapable of understanding my plight. "Why are you so upset?" he asked,
puzzled. "You know that I love you."

"I know, Raul, but this isn't the way I wanted our
relationship to be!" I tried to explain, but my words
failed to express the immensity of my despair.

"Why can't we get married?" he asked again.

"Because God says!" I shot back. "Don't you understand? I've disobeyed God too much already. Now I want
to do things His way. I want the very best He has for me!
Don't you see?"

I knew very well that I had arrived at this moment because my heart and soul had belonged to Raul, and not to the One who rightfully owned me. Raul Ries had distracted my attention from God and His Word.

"No, I don't understand, Sharon. If you love me and I love you, what more is there?"

"There's God's will. And His will is printed on the pages of the Book that I haven't been reading or obeying! His will is everything. It is life! Actually, I shouldn't even be dating you!"

By now I was crying. In spite of everything I was saying, I was quite sure that I would never leave Raul. And I think I knew, even then, that I would suffer grave consequences for it.

Raul pulled the car over and stopped on the side of the freeway.

"Sharon, come here. Let me hold you. Now listen. I love you. I promise . . . I'm going to be a Christian just like you want me to be. But please, just give me some time. I have to learn how, that's all. Honest, I promise. I'll do it for us."

"Raul, what if I'm pregnant? What am I going to do? I've ruined everything and I'm afraid God is going to punish me really bad!" I could hardly talk for weeping.

"Sharon, you're not going to be pregnant. And anyway, if you are, then you'll *have* to marry me!"

In one sense he was joking with me. But the love in his words made me feel secure. He persuaded me that he loved me and that his intentions were right. He convinced me that he would see me through, no matter what.

It wasn't long before his words were put to the test.

The Captain and Me

6

The second we arrived at my house, I jumped out of Raul's red Karman Ghia and ran to the mailbox. Setting my worries aside for the moment, I couldn't wait to see if I had an letters from my mother and sister. They had gone on a missionary journey to Colombia.

Not long before, Shirley had made a serious commitment to God, giving Him her life and her future. Now she had taken a break from school, returning to the country of her birth. The call in her heart had carried her beyond contemporary civilization, to a place where modern conveniences are unknown, where rivers are used for bathing, and where God's lights in the sky and the warm glow of fires are all that illuminate the world.

One year after their wedding, my parents had gone to El Secreto, a missionary vision burning in their heart. There, with the help of some native ranchers, they had hand-carved a mission station at the top of a hill, in the depths of the jungle. All their supplies were carried in by mule train.

I have no memory of the place itself. I do, however, recall our breakneck departure during the religious revolution that occurred there between 1948 and 1958. This uprising was intended to curb Protestant penetration throughout Colombia, and left a trail of atrocities and mass murders in its bloody wake. Mother, Shirley, and I had fled our beloved mission at the point of a rebel's machine gun. Trembling, we climbed into a small D-C3 cargo-passenger airplane whose floor was covered with blood, testifying to the cruelty of the revolutionaries.

Daddy had refused to leave, and so a fanatical military commander temporarily had imprisoned him in a concentration camp. During this violent time, the lives of our schoolchildren were threatened, and then the mission was raided and burned. When they were finished, nothing was left but the 14-inch brick-and-concrete walls. That stark, blackened monument remains to this day. It is a mute reminder of the only steps toward progress ever taken in that primitive region.

It is no secret in our family that Mother left her heart in Colombia. Sometimes she talked about "the place out on the plains where two rivers meet and defy the terrain, where palm trees grow tall and straight, and the wildlife is free, where up on a high hill, a mission sits and waits."

"Someday I will go too," I had silently promised myself.

"A letter! I got a letter from Shirley!" Enraptured, I read it to myself and then aloud to Raul.

March 7, 1968

Dear Sharon,

How are you? Remember all the weight I lost for the airline interviews? Well, I've gained it all back!

All we eat is bread, cooked bananas, and rice. If we're lucky, we get a treat—fishhead soup! Yes, you guessed it—with the eyeballs staring at us.

My legs are all swollen up with mosquito
bites. Now that I don't have malaria, they love
me. Now I understand how itchy and swollen
you used to get when you were a child.

Don't let anyone use my rabbit-hair coat.
PLEASE.

Mother says she appreciates you taking care
of Daddy and the house and that she'll write a
long letter soon with all the details.

Don't study too hard!

Love ya,

Shirley

"Poor sis, she must be a mess! And who would want to
use her fur coat in this heat?" I had to laugh.

I kissed Raul goodbye, walked into the house, threw
myself across my bed, and sobbed. My heart burned
with a desire to be with Shirley, out in the jungle, gain-
ing weight so I could be some mosquito's lunch! I wanted
to go to the mission and hang in a hammock while the
bats flew around the ceiling and the rats ran across the
rafters.

"Oh God," I cried, "forgive me . . . please . . . give me
another chance . . . I want to be a missionary!"

That night before I went to sleep, a picture that Mother
had hung in my room encouraged me. It depicted a
young man carefully steering a ship through the midst of
a fierce storm. Beside him stood Jesus pointing the way.

A prayer spilled out of my troubled spirit: "Be my
Captain, Jesus. Point the way . . . please!"

I opened my Bible to the Psalms. Mother always said
the Psalms would encourage me. I read every one, from
the beginning. Then Psalm 34, verse 19, stopped me
short. Its words penetrated my heart like a sword:
"Many are the afflictions of the righteous, but the Lord
delivereth him out of them all."

I went to sleep thinking about that Scripture, but I found it hard to digest. First of all, I did not feel a bit righteous. Second of all, I did not like the idea that man has many afflictions. I never wanted to suffer again.

Wrestling with the Word of God, I cried myself to sleep.

During the next few weeks, I busied myself with school, cleaning house, and cooking for Daddy and me. I had but one prayer on my lips: "Please God, don't let me be pregnant."

The endless month finally passed. Raul came knocking at my front door early one Saturday morning.

"How's my love?" Raul grabbed me roughly and began to kiss me.

"Raul, come into the kitchen, I have to tell you something." I pushed him away and walked ahead of him. I sat on the stool.

"Raul, I'm pregnant!"

"You're kidding! How do you know?"

"I know, Raul. Believe me, I know!"

Raul impetuously took me in his arms and started swinging me all around the kitchen. "We're going to have a baby. . . . I can't believe it! I'm going to be a daddy! Now you have to marry me!" He said all this in one breath.

I was absolutely shocked. How could he be so happy? My life had all but ended. I was scared to have a baby. I had never included a baby in any of my plans. I didn't even know how to give birth to a baby, much less how to take care of one. Now I couldn't finish school or travel. I wasn't going to be a missionary. Worst of all, I had shamed myself and my parents.

"Raul you don't have to marry me," I retorted. "I'll take care of my baby myself."

"Our baby . . ." he interrupted. ". . . it's our baby and you are going to marry me!"

I think I would have died in my shame had he not answered me in that way. I did want to marry Raul. Not only was I madly in love with him, but I wanted to make things right as soon as possible. I had broken God's law by becoming one flesh with a man who wasn't my husband—a man who didn't know my Lord.

But now I was no longer alone. Through this baby I had tied myself to Raul for life. He would always be my child's father.

Suddenly I had become a family—Raul, the baby, and me. If my baby was to be all that God wanted him to be, his daddy had to know God. I would do whatever was necessary to make us a family in right standing with God. I didn't care if it took forever.

My own determination frightened me, but life without Raul scared me more. I sensed that if I could take Raul home with me, if I could remove him from his environment, I could show him the way to God. I had read in the Bible that an unbelieving husband could be led to God by the lifestyle of a believing wife. It would take wholehearted commitment to God. I could allow absolutely nothing to get between God and me.

I had known all along that there would be ill consequences for my sins. Everybody in the Bible suffered them. But by now I had sincerely repented and I also knew from God's Word that obedience to Him would eventually start producing benefits—the special privileges that one receives when he submits to God's ways. I just needed to learn how to obey Him fully. I would pursue Him with all my heart and soul until I did.

It never entered my mind that our life together wouldn't work out. The God I had come to trust had historically restored His people to Himself whenever they turned to Him. The One I believed in had parted the Red Sea to deliver His children from their adversaries, then had swallowed up the wicked. My Deliverer had closed the mouths of hungry lions when a man of God was thrown into their pit. God was on my side and would remain there as long as I stayed close to him.

One day I tried to communicate these thoughts with Raul. I told him that my family and I lived for God and that I was resolved to teach my children the same values. I wanted my husband-to-be to comprehend what he was getting into. As if in a daze, trying very hard to grasp all that I said, he held me tight and said thoughtfully, "Sharon, I've always wanted a happy home. My dream came true when I met you. You're the only woman I have ever loved, and I will love you forever."

I believed that he would.

The following Sunday, Raul went to the altar to pray at the end of our Bible study. Surely we were on our way to restoration.

Much to my surprise, I experienced incredible strength as I faced the following months. I had to confront pregnancy, wedding plans, and the hardest semester of college finals ever. No matter how overwhelming life became, I could feel the constant nearness of the Captain. I found indescribable comfort in my quiet times with Him.

Although my best dreams had been suddenly drowned in the depths of my disobedience, the hand of the Lord seemed to be steadfastly pointing me in the direction I should take. I felt a peace that passed all my understanding.

I soon realized that I could no longer be in control of my life. Only God could bring order to this disaster. With Him in control I didn't feel it was necessary to hurt my parents, so I didn't tell them or anyone else (except Shirley, once she returned from South America) about my pregnancy. I felt safe with my secret in His confidence.

Raul agreed to secrecy, too. He did tell his mother, however, and she reacted very lovingly, accompanying me to a medical examination. Raul immediately took control and made himself responsible for me. It felt so good. One evening, over dinner at my house, he valiantly asked Daddy for my hand in marriage. Daddy, being a man of few words, said "No," then briefly explained that I needed to finish school, offered Raul some more vegetables, and calmly finished his dinner.

Needless to say, we decided we'd better get married anyway.

I wept over the letter that should have been the happiest I had ever written. It informed Mother and Shirley of our wedding date and plans.

". . . we're going to have a small wedding. We chose your wedding date, Mother, the sixth of July. Come home soon, I need you. I love you, Sharon."

Mother read between the lines. Knowing I was not one to rush into anything, especially marriage, she perceived my dilemma. She and my sister were on their way home anyway, and I was relieved that I hadn't shortened their trip. On their arrival they immediately set about to minimize my pain.

My family never pried into my secret. Raul and I were treated as kindly and affectionately as always. Not one negative word was ever spoken. Mother and Daddy had instructed me explicitly in the ways of God. All that would ever be said concerning the fact that we were spiritually mismatched had already been said. For this I will be eternally indebted to them. During that extremely difficult time, I would not have been able to bear another wound in my already-broken heart.

I owe the same praise to the Ries family. Never have they provoked Raul or me over our unplanned pregnancy.

One night my parents, Raul and I were discussing where we should live once we were married. Mother said, "You must always live alone even if you have to live in one room. Work out all your problems together. Don't involve your families.

"Sharon, don't run home when you and Raul have a disagreement. Put God first in everything you do.

"Raul, the Bible can provide all the guidance you will ever need. Everything is in there. Read it faithfully and you will learn to overcome anything that comes your way."

"Yes, Mrs. Farrel, thank you," Raul nodded very seriously.

Mother's words impressed me deeply, although at that moment I didn't quite realize the importance of their meaning.

"By the way," interrupted Daddy, trying to somehow get a word in, "Mother and I have decided to give you a big wedding. It is a once-in-a-lifetime affair, you know. Sharon, make yourself a beautiful dress because we're inviting the whole world to this wedding!"

I was astounded. I knew my parents could in no way afford to finance a big wedding. It would mean a great sacrifice on their part, and I surely did not deserve it. Their love was like a healing salve on an open wound.

That night before I went to sleep, I prayed, "Dear God, I know that You're disappointed in me. So am I. Please help me make wise decisions. Will You fix the mess I've made out of my life? I promise . . . no I don't want to make any more promises. Can't You just make me do what's right? Yes, that's it. Just cause me to understand Your ways and to do them. And please . . . can I still be a missionary someday?"

Candlelight was the only illumination for the 400 guests who crowded into our church sanctuary. White baskets of green ferns and bouquets of pastel flowers adorned the chapel, filling it with the sweet fragrance of a garden. My bridesmaids wore old-fashioned dresses of rainbow hues.

Sonia glowed in soft mint green. Chrissy, who had demanded a part in the wedding, confidently walked the aisle, lighting the candles. Gowned in pale blue, Shirley never stopped crying till the wedding was through.

Raul's best man, Xavier, stood with Raul's friends who stiffly lined up on the right side of the stage. Most of them, like Raul, were Vietnam veterans, as witnessed by the fierce, angry looks on their faces. I was hoping that something would happen to make them smile. It never did. I have the pictures to prove it.

As soon as my cousin Janet finished singing "O Promise Me," the processional music began. On my head a cluster of orange blossoms held a long, pure silk veil in place. It softly draped over my face and entirely covered my organdy dress. A real cameo set in 14-carat gold accented the high, lace-trimmed neckline. The dress was all that I had imagined it could be. I was not.

I'd never felt so safe walking with Daddy as I did at that special moment. Though I was weak, arm in arm with him, his strength held me up. I fully understood why fathers have to give their daughters away. If they didn't, no bride would ever make it down the aisle.

Daddy struggled to say just the right words. He squeezed my hand. "You will be all that God wants you to be. Don't worry." From the back of the church, I could see Mother's tear-filled eyes. Once more they instructed me. No words were needed. I could read her thoughts.

"Sharon, I've tried to do my best. God gave you to me. I gave you God's Word. I know you're going to make it. Your life was endangered at birth, and I promised God I would name you Sharon Faith if He would save your life. I also asked Him not to give me any children who would not serve Him. So, Sharon Faith, follow Him and serve Him. Be married to Christ. I give you to Him. I won't interfere."

A tearful smile tried to form on my lips as I watched her. She was so gentle, so controlled. I knew that her strength came from God. She trusted only in Him.

By now I could see Raul clearly. His eyes were seeking mine. He was more splendid than all the princes in every storybook I had ever read. He was the fulfillment of every desire I'd ever had. I was his bride and he was my groom forever.

Radiant with confidence, he stood and waited, so very unaware of what he was getting into. The first two rows of seats right in front of him contained my family. I knew they would be praying, that day and every day that followed.

"Who gives this woman to be married to this man?" I heard the voice of Pastor Green.

Daddy gave me away, then moved to the altar to say the marriage vows with us.

I was vaguely troubled to see that Raul was paying very little attention to the ceremony. Instead, he spent those sacred minutes whispering to me, telling me how beautiful I looked. During the ring exchange, under his breath, I even heard him compliment my nails!

Despite his lack of interest, I managed to seriously and devotedly struggle through the vows. Raul's distractions invoked an unexpected urging deep within my being. I found myself saying my vows to Jesus rather than to Raul.

"Whither Thou goest I will go," I whispered to the Lord. "Whither Thou lodgest I will lodge. Your people shall be my people and Your God shall be my God. . . . I promise to love, cherish, and obey You."

All at once I could scarcely repeat the words. I became enveloped in a warmth that started from the top of my head and wrapped itself lovingly around me. It was a sensation unlike any I had ever experienced.

"I present to you Mr. and Mrs. Raul Andrew Ries." Pastor Green ended the ceremony by introducing us to the congregation. As we walked down the aisle, a soft voice that I had never heard before whispered to my heart, "I will never leave you."

I don't know how, but I recognized the Captain's voice. I had the unexpected perception that I was glowing. I felt virgin and pure. I was forgiven.

No matter what lay ahead, my future would always be warmed by God's presence. I would never leave Him.

And He would never leave me—for better or for worse.

Ship of Dreams

7

My favorite fantasy never foretold the pleasure and satisfaction that Raul initially brought into my life. Childhood hopes and dreams suddenly and painlessly vanished as he became my yesterday, my today, and my tomorrow. My world became wholeheartedly his.

I genuinely respected the way he accepted his manly responsibilities. Raul Ries was determined to succeed in life, and had the natural ability to do so. He worked hard, and was faithful to me both as husband and breadwinner. No doubt remained—he obviously loved me with all his heart. I wanted nothing but to be his, "to have and to hold from this day forward until death do us part."

By the third day of our marriage, Raul had me nestled into a cozy one-bedroom apartment in Anaheim. It was situated halfway between Camp Pendleton and our hometown. We furnished it with a king-size mattress from Raul's folks, a dinette set from mine, and carloads of wedding gifts. All we lacked was a refrigerator. It wasn't long before Daddy appeared on our doorstep with one that was tiny and loud, but served its purpose very well. It was probably one of the first refrigerators ever made, but Raul modernized it by spray painting it bright yellow.

Raul had very little time to spare, but whatever time he had we spent together. Sometimes he bribed the night guard at the base and came home to spend the night with me. His restrictions were puzzling to me since other Marines went home during the week. Raul explained that it was because of tight security at Pendleton. It didn't matter to me, because I thought it was delightfully romantic that he would sneak out to see me.

In August, the heat kept me up late. Many nights I sat under the stars, waiting for Raul. As I gazed into the vastness of the heavens, my thoughts focused on God and His greatness. Who was I that He should take any thought of me? And yet He did.

I contemplated how Jesus, who was part of God Himself, had left His throne in the heavens at the will of His Father. He had made Himself of no reputation, taking the form of a servant, made in the likeness of man. He had humbled Himself, obeying His Father by submitting to a criminal's death—death on a cross.

In doing this, Jesus took the blame for all our past, present, and future sins. He became our sacrifice, so that we would never have to be punished for our transgressions. The King of kings and Lord of lords was beaten for His subjects.

No matter what I had done, my heavenly Father saw me as a righteous child because of Jesus' death and resurrection. In the Bible I had read that those who believe on Jesus and confess their sins, receiving Him as Lord and Savior, are free from mental condemnation as well as eternal damnation. I had heard this teaching all my life, but had never quite understood it until now. "Who will bring any charge against those whom God has chosen?" Paul wrote in Romans 8:33 (NIV). "It is God who justifies [makes pure]." The awesomeness of these thoughts made my heart explode with joy.

On the nights Raul came home, he would rush in shortly after midnight. Invariably, he would snatch my attention away from all else. We'd stay up half the night. I would try to communicate my innermost thoughts toward God. He'd tell me about all his plans.

"I'm a fighter. I'll always be one. I want to become a professional kung fu instructor. I'd like to open up my own studio someday."

My only desire was to be Raul's wife, to help him unfold his vision. I would fall asleep dreaming about how wonderful it was all going to be.

Four months after our wedding, Raul charged through the front door, laughing hilariously. He picked me up in his arms and shouted. "Sharon, my dear, you are looking at a free man! They gave me an honorable discharge! An honorable discharge! Can you believe that?"

"Raul, why are you getting discharged two years early? And why shouldn't it be honorable? You fought in Vietnam, didn't you? You were wounded twice. You almost lost your life!" I was confused.

"I'll tell you why. Because the therapist at the base doesn't like me at all. That's why he never lets me come home." He handed me the doctor's analysis. I read the report and couldn't believe how absurd it was.

"This doctor is nuts!" I agreed. "He doesn't know what he's talking about. He says your outbursts of anger caused you to be released from the Marines. I don't think I've ever seen you angry, Raul. You don't have an angry bone in your body!"

Raul's expression became serious. He looked very guilty.

"So did you get angry?" Fear rippled inside me. I remembered the fight at school that had kept him from being my escort when I was a homecoming princess. How well did I know this man? Besides, I was a little disappointed. I'd been harboring a secret wish that we might be stationed in a foreign country some day.

"Oh, you know." He flippantly waved my concern aside. "I just got a little mad when those guys tried to get me to do dumb stuff like polish my shoes and brass. Nobody cared about polished brass in Nam, I can tell you that!"

Within days of Raul's discharge he was working nights at the bank where his mother was employed. Soon he was going to college full-time during the day. Busy as he was, however, he would find his way home whenever he had a few minutes. I thrived on his love for me.

On my Mother's forty-sixth birthday, December 21, 1968, Raul found himself driving 100 m.p.h. on the San Bernardino Freeway. A call at work had informed him that his wife was about to deliver his first-born child. He drove all the way to Anaheim with his emergency lights flashing. While the new father was sick to his stomach out by the Fairview Hospital trash cans, little Raul Andrew Jr. and I busied ourselves quickly pushing his 9 lb. 14 oz. body through the birth canal. At last he was safe in my arms.

That first birth was a frightening experience for me. I was afraid of the pain I was experiencing. I was concerned with the awesome responsibility of being a mother. And I was wondering what kind of a dad Raul would be. As soon as I was left alone with my newborn son, I held him straight up in the air and gave him back to his Maker.

"God, I give You this child forever. If he's not going to love you, take him back. I don't want the agony of having a child who will not love You." I determined right then that as long as I had breath to breathe I would instruct this child in the ways of God. In this way I would follow the example of my mother and grandmother. They were still giving instruction to me and my sister.

Mother had the flu, so Shirley, who was home from college, was elected to help me take care of my baby.

Before I did anything about mothering the little fellow, I diligently read all the directions in the baby book. Meanwhile, Shirley disinfected the entire house and boiled all the nipples and pacifiers to pieces.

Although we were a sad pair of nurses, Raul Andrew lived up to the meaning of his name: "strong, gentle commander." He survived this life-threatening episode quite happily. Raul Sr. absolutely adored him. "You look like a little priest, buddy." He gently rubbed his baby's fuzzy-brown head.

"Isn't our little boy the most perfect creation of God you've ever seen?

"Yeah . . ." Raul answered, an inquisitive look on his face.

I had never been so content. My husband and son seemed to be the cure for all that had ever ailed me. For that all-too-brief period of time, loving and taking care of them removed the emptiness from my existence. I gladly poured myself into them. As far as I was concerned, nothing else on this earth had any comparable value.

The fog rolled in that first Christmas Eve, and Raul didn't notice the tiny, lighted Christmas tree I had placed in the window to surprise him. We ate by candlelight while Raulie slept next to the manger scene, under the twinkling lights. When he awakened for his feeding, we took our first family picture. I had on a new robe. Raulie wore the too-big red hat my dad had given him "to wear home from the hospital." Raul sat proudly on his new weight-lifting bench, flexing his Marine Corps muscles.

The day after Christmas, against my will, we packed our few belongings and moved to Covina, near our hometown. Raul wanted to be near his friends and family. I just wanted to be with him and visit our families occasionally. In Anaheim, we had been completely alone. No friends had disturbed our privacy, no telephone had interrupted our dialogue. The move to Covina altered our tranquil family atmosphere into a far different environment.

Within hours of our arrival, Raul began to phone his old high school buddies.

Several days later, he was spending most of his free time with them.

Within weeks, his disposition began to change radically.

My happy dream was over. I was alone again. The haunting emptiness had returned.

The one good result of our move was that my parents lived nearby. This gave me the opportunity to go back to school part-time. Mother was fascinated by Raulie, and delighted in spending a few hours with him each week.

But matters with Raul were not so pleasant. It seemed as if he had exchanged his loving, exciting personality for an altogether different one. Although he still cherished Raulie, he was suddenly disinterested in family life. He became slothful around the house, leaving all the work to me—inside and out. Previously we had been going to church together. Now, if I mentioned going, it annoyed him.

His interests were now self-centered. If I intruded on his plans, he spoke to me with disrespect and started pushing me around. When I refused to go partying with him, he became angry. Before long he began to use filthy language. It hurt me deeply to be called such degrading names. I had been raised in a home where words such as "stupid" and "dummy" were considered vulgar. His words were far worse than any I had ever heard. Because of our lives taking such opposite roads, fighting became a regular habit. With each disagreement, his disrespect and his manhandling of me got worse. He always apologized; therefore, we were constantly making up. I loved him so much. Forgiving him came easy, but when I was alone I cried for hours. I was mourning the loss of another dream.

Raul had started taking professional kung fu lessons four nights a week, as well as on Saturdays. Many times he told me about the fights he got into. He revealed to me that he had been in prison in the Marines for fighting. Now I understood why he hadn't been able to come home to me all those nights.

I noticed something very disturbing in all Raul's stories. No matter what happened, it was always the other person's fault. His irresponsible attitude frightened me. I had trouble sleeping.

One night he came in wild-eyed, his shirt bloody and torn. In my view, he was like a little boy who kept getting in neighborhood fights. I sat down with him the way Mother had always done with us when we were bad little girls.

"Raul, we're adults now. We need to change our ways. I've done that, haven't I? God has given a new life to you, Raulie, and me. Let's love each other and have fun together, okay?"

Raul flared immediately. He didn't like being corrected in any way. "Don't you tell me how to live my life! I'll live it my way. If you don't like it, get out!"

The massive lump in my throat forced me to whisper. "Honey, please . . . please don't say that."

"Are you telling me to forget about my friends? Now you know why I didn't want to get involved with you in high school. I didn't want any woman telling me what to do! I had my friends before you came into my life, and you'll never take their place! Just do your housework and take care of my son. That's all women are good for anyway!" He was still shouting as he threw a kitchen chair at me and stormed out the door. I could hear him outside muttering, "Women! They're all alike! Nag, nag nag!"

I wept all night. The next morning I found a long-stemmed yellow rose in a crystal vase beside the kitchen sink. Next to it was a note. "My dearest little redhead that I love so much, I know I have hurt you really bad. Please forgive me. Raul A. Ries." I did.

We had been so much in love, and now we had nothing in common. He had lost interest in our home and in God. After going to a few of his parties, I realized we lived in two different worlds. I thought back to the unexpected encounter at the neighborhood market, years before, when Raul had lied to me. Something deep inside had warned me to run. Now I could quote the Scripture by heart that I should have remembered that day:

> Be ye not unequally yoked together with unbelievers: for what fellowship hath righteousness with unrighteousness? And what communion hath light with darkness? (2 Corinthians 6:14).

Light has nothing in common with darkness. That much I had learned.

Although Raul and I were practicing birth control, I discovered that I was pregnant when Raulie was six months old. I like to think that this baby sang songs of comfort to me during my pregnancy, because the thought of this child helped to turn my eyes off my troubles and onto God and His abundant favor toward me. Raul didn't like the name Shane ("beloved of God") at the time, but he agreed to it anyway. Today Shane is a songwriter whose tunes fill our home daily with peace and joy.

When the nurse first brought Shane to me for feeding, I lifted him up to the heavens and prayed:

"I give him back to You, to mold within Your hands. Take him back from where he came if he's not going to honor You with his life."

After two more difficult semesters in college, I had to drop out. It was a full-time job taking care of my boys.

While we were faced with our own difficulties, Raul's family was also engaged in continuing warfare. This involved in-laws from both sides of their family. According to Raul, it had all begun the day his parents got married. Papi was an alcoholic, Josie the product of a confrontational home life.

Each person in the family fought against another, taking one point of view one day, then changing sides as new circumstances arose. It was nearly impossible to get close to any of the families without being dragged into a quarrel.

Raul's mother and father were very hard workers who really cared about their four children. Unfortunately, they didn't have the love of God controlling their turbulent emotions.

I tried to reach out to them by baking birthday cakes for everyone, sewing, and helping to decorate their house. I thought maybe I could show them how to love each other. I failed, and the war raged on. Before long Raul's family turned against me, too. This occurred because they didn't like the fact that I was teaching Chrissy about God. She wanted to spend more and more time at our house.

Chrissy filled our home with dancing, laughter, and music. The boys and I never tired of her company. When Mother had been silently sorrowing over my premarital pregnancy, the Lord had comforted her with words from Psalm 113:9: "He maketh the barren woman to keep house, and to be a joyful mother of children."

Chrissy and I lived this verse in the midst of the storm that sometimes swirled around us. We did everything together. We went to church, sewed, cleaned, shopped, and cried together. She suffered from her family's abuse, and I suffered from Raul's. She became the first American friend I could really relate to.

During those days, Raul and his dad would come at each other like two raging bulls. Every time we visited his parents, Raul found himself defending my beliefs, even though he didn't accept them for himself. Raul didn't care if he ever saw his mother and father again. To him they represented pain and, as it was, he could hardly handle his own inner torment.

One night I persuaded Raul to attend one of his family's birthday parties. He didn't want to go, and once we were there, I was so sorry I hadn't listened to him. As usual, a fight broke out after Papi and Raul offended each other. Our little family fled, literally running for the car.

Raul began kicking me as he wildly drove down the street. "You filthy witch! Why don't you just stay out of my life? Why don't you leave me alone? You've ruined my life with your religion and your stupid family."

I clutched Raulie and Shane in my arms, petrified as the car swerved from one side of the road to the other.

"Raul, you are my life!" I hysterically screamed back at him. "Our boys are my life. Don't ask me to get out. I won't! Don't you understand? I'm here to stay!"

Shipwrecked

8

"I'm here to stay!"

The words echoed and reechoed in my mind. I was amazed by what I had said. Although my fear of Raul grew with every passing day, I was committed to seeing my family through. I remembered a Bible verse that says, "God hates divorce." I hated it too. The thought of the boys having another father sickened me.

When we got home, drained by his emotional outburst, Raul went straight to bed. After tucking my two little sleepyheads under their blankets, I put my hands on each of their heads and prayed. "Father, please erase this night from their memories. In Jesus' Name, Amen."

I grabbed my robe and a blanket and went into the bathroom to "pray through." "That's when you pray till you get an answer from God," Grandma Kopp had taught us grandchildren.

Decades before, after she received a 14-page letter from Grandpa, asking her hand in marriage, her father had told her to "pray through." She was in a desperate state. She didn't love the young man who wanted to marry her. After her time of prayer, she received her answer, and I could still hear her describing it.

"I became filled with love for your grandpa, and that pure, divine love has never failed me."

That terrible night I needed to receive the same kind of love Grandma had. Mine was running out real fast. As I wept bitter tears, I grabbed my Bible and beat on it with my fist. "I know the answer is in here, Lord! Please, please show me what to do!"

"I got my eyes on an unbeliever," I told God. "I disobeyed You. I sinned. You forgave me and gave me peace, but now I'm reaping the results of my sins. I understand! But, how long do I stay with Raul before it starts doing damage to the boys? I have a responsibility to them too. Your Word says to train up a child in the way he should go so when he is old, he won't depart from it. You also said, 'Suffer the little children to come unto me, and forbid them not: for of such is the kingdom of heaven.' Lord, my children are learning ways that are not Yours," I cried to my heavenly Father. "Am I hindering them from coming to You by staying with Raul?"

I opened the Bible, hurriedly flipping the pages from beginning to end. All at once a verse marked in bright red caught my eye: "Many are the afflictions of the righteous, but the Lord delivereth him out of them all."

"Not that one again." I slammed my Bible shut. "I'll just sit here and wait."

The verse kept repeating itself in my brain. I heard it over and over again. I began to understand. I had my answer, and it came to me straight from God's Word.

I thought about what the words meant. God's people suffer afflictions, but the Lord delivers us from all of them. At that moment I understood that I would suffer a lot. Everybody did. The point was, I didn't have to worry. The love of God would get me through! My bitter tears were dried. Joy and love flowed from my heart in a prayer of thanksgiving.

"Thank you, Lord, for giving me Your unfailing love

for Raul. Save him for me, please. I need him to be my
lover, friend, and husband."

My parents never knew the extent of my pain. I never
told them. Sundays, when they saw me without Raul,
they understood that something was wrong. They never
meddled in my life, but always offered encouragement
and Scriptures that gave me hope. Like everyone else,
they had had their own problems. But they had always
worked things out privately without involving Shirley
and me.

Raul's parents were under the impression that I dominated their son. I decided to let them believe whatever
they wanted. Explanations were futile—any conversation could start another conflict. In any case, they always
seemed to be mad at us. Raul and I felt forsaken by them.
One day I ran across a promise from the Book of Psalms:
"When my father and my mother forsake me, then the
Lord will take me up" (Psalm 27:10).

And that's exactly what he did! Just when we needed
them, God provided an extra Mom and Pop who showed
up at all our family events. No one could take the place of
Raul's parents, but Uncle Gayle and Aunt Daphyne,
unaware of Raul's and my distress, stood in the gap.

Uncle Gayle was one of Daddy's twin brothers, and
Auntie Phene was my dad's only sister. Raul really cherished both of them, which was unusual for him. Santa
never came to our house on Christmas. It was Uncle
Gayle, sent by Jesus, bringing the kinds of gifts children
wish for and parents can't afford. He was the first and
last person I've ever heard affectionately call my husband "Raulie." Somehow he even got away with filling
our garage with yard-sale merchandise. He is still special
in our hearts although he has moved back East and we
seldom see him.

Auntie Phene admired Raul so much; her face always
lit up when she saw him. She came bearing boxes of
fabrics that provided our family with much-needed

clothing. Besides all that, we received buckets of love, hugs, and an endless stream of snapshots. A few years ago she retired and moved up to Northern California. We communicate by telephone, shed tears, and I always lack the words to express to her how special she is to me.

In spite of occasional moments of gentleness, by the time another year had passed, my relationship with Raul had become unbearable. I was so weary. One Sunday I woke up to a beautiful southern California morning. Rain had cleared the sky, and the mountains and foot-hills were laden with snow. I was on my way out the front door with the boys. Raul, who usually went dirt biking on weekends, had stayed home.

The phone began to ring. I didn't want to answer it. Raul was already in a rage because I'd asked him to accompany us to church and then spend the day with us. When I'd suggested it, he'd given me his usual verbal abuse. "You are boring. Read my lips," Raul had said to me as he grabbed my face and shoved it too close to his and spelled out b-o-r-i-n-g. "Get that? Now get out of here. Go with your church friends. Out! Out! Out!" he screamed as he pushed me out the bedroom door. It was so humiliating to be thrown around like rubbish. His filthy words always hurt—like knives cutting at my insides. Now I was trying to get out of the house before my day was completely ruined.

"Pick up the phone, you big nag!" he yelled from the bedroom. "Maybe then you'll have someone to listen to you!"

The phone kept ringing. "Hello?" I finally answered, fighting back the tears.

"Sharie, aren't you coming to church?" Daddy's voice sounded worried. "I've been waiting outside to help you in with the boys and the diaper bag."

"I don't know, Daddy," my voice quivered.

"What's the matter? What's happening over there anyway?"

Just then, Raul marched into the kitchen, grabbed my face with his hand, and shoved the telephone receiver into it repeatedly, bouncing my head against the wall.

I screamed hysterically into the phone, "Raul's hurting me, Daddy!. . . Daddy?" The phone went dead.

Raul released me. He blamed me for the entire incident.

"You witch! You like to get tough, but when you can't handle it you cry like a baby. What's your Dad going to think now? You're making him think that I beat you up."

Raul never admitted to himself that he hurt me. Abusive people usually don't.

"You're an idiot," he continued, "and everybody knows it, too. My friends, my family, the people I work with . . ."

"Raul, the boys are going to hear you . . . please stop."

He threw me onto the kitchen floor and yelled louder, "I hope they do hear so they know what a nag their mom is. Nag, nag, nag, that's all you do!"

Raul called me a nag whenever I asked him to take out the trash, mow the lawn, or do anything around the house. It hurt so deeply. At the time, I thought it was up to me to remind him of his duties as a husband, and so I did. I hadn't yet learned that it was better to do things for myself than to try to motivate him.

Besides, whether I asked him once or ten times, he always responded the same way. This was particularly true when I so much as mentioned God or church.

I have learned from other people that some women are accused of nagging even if they are silent. Sometimes their godly witness speaks more loudly than words.

I got up and ran out of the kitchen to see where the boys were. They had gone out the front door and were happily sitting in a mud puddle wearing their Sunday best. I held them both very tight.

"Mommy loves you two very much."

"Me too, Mommy," said Shane, sweetly pressing his dirty cheek against mine."

"Me too!" echoed Raulie as he leaped out of my arms and did a couple of somersaults on the front lawn.

Neither had seen nor heard anything. I was so thankful to God.

Daddy arrived. Without any display of emotion, he asked if the boys and I wanted to go for a ride. As we drove along, he said to me, "Trust in God; this will all pass. Don't give up! One of these days Raul will surrender to God. He's a good man, Sharon."

The faith in his words pierced my heart. I returned home, hoping to find a way to go on. There I found a red rose laying on my pillow with a note on it that read, "My little freckled nose that I'm so in love with, will you forgive me? Please? Your Lover, Raul A. Ries." I didn't.

I was disgusted with his notes and his roses. They meant nothing to me. I threw the rose in the wastepaper basket in our bedroom so he could see it. I stored the note with all the rest of them in the little green box I kept in my closet.

The jovial spirit that had once drawn me to Raul was now obscured by his anger. Although he was an intelligent, good-looking man, his temper always caused him to act like a fool. The manliness and control that had once strengthened his character withered under the intense heat of his fury. How quickly his emotions could debilitate him! Wherever he went, he stirred up strife.

I could never defend myself against his words by answering back; it only made matters worse. Raul could quickly think of a more degrading thing to say. Then his retort would repeat itself over and over again in my conscience, tearing at the foundations of my self-respect. Naturally, I didn't dare to fight back physically. I had learned that people who have no self-control prey on the weak.

But, hurt as I was, I wanted Raul to hear how he sounded. I wanted him to hurt the way I did. One night, during a terrible argument, I looked straight into his eyes and said words I had never spoken to him before.

"I hate you. I hate the sight of you. I don't know how I ended up with you. It makes me sick when you make love to me!"

He shouted something back, but I saw the hurt. It was deep. I had reopened some past, unhealed wound. Worse yet, my words hadn't even been true. I had lied in order to hurt Raul. I could never do it again. The depth that a person suffers abuse of any form—whether it be physical, verbal, neglect, or rejection—is totally dependent on the treatment that the individual has received throughout his life. If a person has been highly respected, deeply loved, and always encouraged, a seemingly simple phrase such as "you make me sick" has an incredible, disastrous emotional affect on him. Just as I had hurt Raul deeply, even his "light" abuse tortured my mind to the same degree that his most vulgar statements or worst physical treatment did.

How easily I had learned his ways. Wasn't my heart just as wicked as his? I knew from God's Word that a "gentle answer turns away wrath, but a harsh word stirs up anger." I, too, was choosing to war, to inflict pain.

The outside woodwork had needed a coat of paint ever since we had bought the house two years before. After asking Raul several times (nagging as he called it), I decided to do the painting myself. It was very cold outside, but I was enjoying myself immensely. When Raul drove up after work, he commented on what a nice job I was doing. I noticed he was home very early.

"Guess what? I'm going to open a kung fu studio right around the corner."

"That's great!" I jumped off the ladder so he could tell me more.

"How are you going to work it out with your job?" I asked.

"You're going to go to work and help me!"

I was horrified. There wasn't anything on earth—not clothes, furniture, or even vacations—that could have ever enticed me to leave Raulie and Shane. Who would read them their stories? Teach them Spanish? Pray for their hurts? No one understood their individual strengths and weaknesses like I did. Who else would cry with them or laugh at their silly jokes? Only I could love them the way they deserved to be loved.

I carefully explained it all to Raul. He didn't change his mind.

The next day he informed me that his hours had been cut unexpectedly at the market where he was a checker. He had changed jobs when we moved. "Now you'll have to get a job."

He wasn't a very convincing liar.

The day I threw the rose away, I began to harden my heart against my husband. I threw a few more away. Then he stopped giving them to me.

I no longer wanted to forgive Raul. And I decided I didn't want to suffer anymore, either. I was exhausted—emotionally, physically, and spiritually.

Over and over, I flipped through the pages of the Book. I could find no answer that suited me. I prayed, cried, and crawled into my bed. Before I found a job, I started sleeping in the middle of the day, every day. I was trying to forget my anguish, and being awake meant being aware.

I was lost in a sea of desperation with no lighthouse in sight. Hope was gone. I had finally shipwrecked.

The Captain? I don't know. I didn't think about Him much anymore.

Swimming Against the Current

9

I dragged myself out of bed. Emotionally drained, I felt as if I hadn't slept. The boys were already awake, playing in their toy-cluttered bedroom. I stood at their door unnoticed, watching as they energetically participated in full-scale combat, throwing toys back and forth from one bed to the other. Red, white, and blue wooden Civil War knickknacks that were supposed to be decorating their dressers were scattered all over the carpet.

Raul had escaped with his friends for the weekend, leaving me with a house that needed cleaning, bills to be paid, yard work, food shopping, and two never-resting, mess-making little boys who required constant attention. Where had Raul said he was going this time? The prospect of another weekend without his help or companionship crippled me.

In spite of everything, I ached to be with my husband. Yet the faint hope for change in Raul's behavior had all but vanished. All around me the world was beaming with life, but I was only a spectator. I was enclosed in darkness, and I couldn't find my way out.

Mother was on her way to pick up the boys. She would

take them out for a day of fun, and as soon as they were
gone, I would go right back to bed until they returned. I
did not want to deal with my circumstances anymore.
This was my way of escape. Sleep made the lonely weekends pass more quickly.

"Good morning, boys! I love you," I hoped my cheerful tone would cover up my distress.

"Where's Daddy, Mommy?" asked two-year-old Raulie. He was always aware of everything.

"Gone with his friends, love, but you're going to have
a fun day with Banna!" I changed the subject rapidly,
hoping he wouldn't pursue it. He did.

"I wanna see Daddy, Mommy!" he insisted.

"We'll go to kung fu with him this week, okay?"

The best way for us to see Raul was to follow him
wherever he went. Despite his disinterest in home life,
he was proud to have his boys around him. He just
didn't want them to divert him from the activities he
craved.

Mother arrived, her van fully equipped with an assort-
ment of plastic soldiers, little pieces of wood, rubber
bands, ice cream sticks, and plastic egg cartons. These
would aid in building dams in the mountain streams,
and constructing rafts for floating soldiers.

"Sharon, why don't you go with us? You need a break,
honey. The fresh air will be good for you."

"Oh, no thanks. I really need to stay home and get
some things done."

"Oh, by the way, I left a letter from Chile on your
kitchen counter! It came yesterday," she yelled out the
window as she and the boys drove away, waving goodbye.

My heart skipped a beat. A letter from Chile?

It had been four years since I had heard from any of my
friends there. A longing for my home country seized my
heart once more. The envelope lay on the messy counter,

next to a sinkful of dirty dishes. I recognized the hand-writing immediately. It hadn't changed much in the last few years. It was from Fernando.

Up in my closet, in the little green box, I still had all of his letters. Tears welled up inside. I realized that I hadn't even told him I was married. How could I explain all that had happened to me? We had promised each other, year after year, that we would someday be together.

All the curtains were drawn, and the house was dark. I walked slowly down the hall and into my bedroom. After crawling into bed, I read the letter several times.

Dear Sharon,

I can't remember why our correspondence stopped. Probably the distance between us made it impossible for our relationship to develop.

There is one thing very clear in my mind. Our ongoing wish was to see each other some-day, somehow. I still cherish that desire and I hope you do too. I believe that the moment has finally arrived, as I have won a scholarship to New York. I know that it is a long way from Los Angeles, but maybe we can meet somewhere in between. How could life be so cruel as to keep us apart once more?

Loving you as always,

Fernando

I began to weep, quietly but deeply. I didn't resort to the Bible as I always had before when I was in distress. I wanted to feel this moment. I wanted to savor what could have been had I not gotten involved with Raul. Had Fernando been the man God had chosen for me? Why else was the past knocking at my heart's door, mocking me?

I held his letter on my chest, next to my heart. The passions that had always steered my life challenged me to follow their urgings once more. I remembered Chile, the mission, and my childhood love. Dreamer that I am, I drifted back into what once had been my favorite fantasy. It had only changed a little.

Instead of disembarking from a ship, I was getting off an airplane in New York. I was wearing a white tailored suit and, as always, my long hair was blowing·in the wind. I was meeting Fernando. He was softly kissing my cheek . . .

The dream came to an abrupt end.

I was married and had two children that I adored! Fernando was single, in love with life, pursuing his career. Why would he want me anymore?

Despite the cold realities, I couldn't bear to answer the letter. I wanted too much to be with him, to forget that I had ever met Raul. It was like a dream come true. The prince had reappeared to rescue the princess. She had been locked up in the dungeon of the castle and abused by the wicked sorcerer. Was this my magical entrance to happiness, just like in the fairy tales? Or was it another deception?

My emotions had gotten me into my present mess. I didn't want to be led astray again.

Somehow, I remembered God. I wanted to make this decision according to what He said, not according to what the urgings of my heart dictated. "It's a dream, that's all!" A tiny thought convinced me. I put the letter under my pillow and went to sleep, hoping to hush my wayward thoughts.

The following days found me opening my Bible frequently, searching for guidance. Unfortunately, my habitual thinking patterns always interfered with my reading. I was desperately trying to fill my emptiness with fantasy—dreams of the future or memories of the past.

The by-product of my daydreams was the most intense self-pity I had ever experienced.

My focus was entirely on myself. It was causing me to lose sight of all that held any value. My home, my sons, their father, and the love that I had once had for him no longer seemed important.

And now I was dealing with the much-dreaded job Raul had imposed upon me. It was another nightmare. Because I was bilingual, I had landed a secretarial position for which I was totally unskilled. I received minimum wage and, due to my inexperience, my boss didn't like me at all.

All that was overshadowed by my agony over not being with my boys. The first time I took them to the babysitter, Raul went along. He wanted to show me how easy it was to leave them.

"No problem, you'll see. It won't be a problem at all," he confidently assured me.

Shane and Raulie were more fluent in Spanish than English, so I gave the sitter a translated list of words they often used so she could understand what they were saying. We prayed, and kissed each other goodbye. Then, to my horror, I stood helplessly as Raul shoved screaming little Shane back from the front door and quickly closed it on his face!

Driving away, I saw two little blond-haired, brown-eyed boys pressing their noses against the sitter's living room windows.

"They'll get used to it after a while." Raul thought he was comforting me.

"I never will," I whispered under my breath.

At first, I went to read Bible stories to them during my lunch hour. But after a few days the babysitter asked me not to. "They won't stop crying after you leave, and it keeps them from taking their naps." After that I spent lunch alone.

I hated Raul. I realized he was a hard worker, but he made me feel like an object, useful only to help him achieve his goals. While he studied and practiced martial arts, enjoying himself thoroughly, I did the unpleasant menial duties seven days a week. Worst of all, I was being denied time with the boys during some of the most important learning years of their lives.

Trying to work out my problems confused me. Some days I felt that our difficulties were all my fault. I deserved what I had. It was during those days that I suffered with severe depression. Other days, I was convinced everything was Raul's fault. I would be flooded with anger and would entertain vindictive ideas. Either way, I was living in a sick state of mind, and I didn't like it.

Instead of pursuing God, I couldn't get my eyes off myself and my troubles. No longer did I see God's guidance. I just kept telling Him I was sorry and asking Him to help me. "Show me the way out!" I prayed, day after day.

One morning I woke up with a very clear awareness, a change in my perspective which quickly led me to a life-changing decision. A Bible verse broke through the smothering cloud of depression. I had listened to it countless times in my childhood. I could almost hear the thundering voices of various South American preachers echoing it:

> Be not deceived; God is not mocked: for whatsoever a man soweth, that shall he also reap. For he that soweth to his flesh shall of the flesh reap corruption; but he that soweth to the Spirit shall of the Spirit reap life everlasting. And let us not be weary in well doing: for in due season we shall reap, if we faint not (Galatians 6:7-9).

I had planted thousands of selfish, self-pitying thoughts in my mind: thoughts about killing myself, finding another man, running away, and living for myself. Those wicked and destructive concepts had corrupted me.

It dawned on me that my dreams were not real. They were nothing more than mini-escapes from reality, encompassing only a fleeting moment in eternity. My dreams were not true, and they should never be brought to pass unless they were part of the Creator's infinite plan for my future.

For me, indifference toward anyone was not normal. Now, through unhealthy thinking, my hatred for Raul was rapidly fading into indifference toward him. The constant quarreling in his family, causing verbal attacks on us, had also made me indifferent toward them.

Emotional detachment is, in some ways, worse than hate, for when you hate you still feel hurt. Indifference produces no feelings. It is like death. My thoughts were bringing death to those around me and to myself.

Love was dying in my heart.

I needed desperately to start planting God's thoughts in my mind. I wanted to cultivate my hardened heart. I longed to experience life in a way I had never known before. Most of all, I could not allow myself to grow weary—no matter what—in doing the right things. True, life was tough. But God had promised a good result—a happy harvest.

It had been a couple of months since I had received Fernando's letter. It was time to answer it. I knew it would be one of the hardest things I had ever done, but I wanted to obey God. And sometimes obedience to Him isn't easy.

I wrote to Fernando, but hid all the passion that was torturing my mind. How I yearned for this diligent young suitor to defiantly come and rescue me! I craved his forgiveness, tenderness, and companionship. In my letter, however, I told him that I was married and had two lovely children. I invited him to come to our home. Couldn't we at least be friends?

I lived on hope while I awaited his answer. I really believed that my letter would be the beginning of something wonderful—an adult friendship, a renewed contact with Chile. He never wrote back.

Disillusionment gradually kidnapped me again. Fernando was gone forever, and forever was a long, long time to be unloved.

After a few days of trying to climb out of my pit alone, I set the alarm extra early one morning, declaring war against my misery. Determined to change my self-pitying thought patterns, I looked up the word "think" and "mind" in a Bible concordance. The first thing I needed to learn was how to stop my sick thinking from interfering with God's thoughts. Here's what I found:

> The weapons of our warfare are not carnal, but mighty through God to the pulling down of strongholds: casting down imaginations, and every high thing that exalteth itself against the knowledge of God, and bringing into captivity every thought to the obedience of Christ (2 Corinthians 10:4,5).

How exciting! With God's help, I could pull down any stronghold in my life. My imagination was a stubborn one, but He was able to help me destroy the thoughts that governed my life and exalted themselves above His. He alone knew how to take those thoughts into captivity, making Himself the rightful monarch of my consciousness.

I meditated upon the verses I was finding. Another one told me how to get started on my new adventure in thinking:

> Be careful [anxious] for nothing: but in everything by prayer and supplication with

thanksgiving let your requests be made known unto God. And the peace of God, which passes all understanding, shall keep your hearts and minds through Christ Jesus. Finally, brethren, whatsoever things are true, whatsoever things are honest, whatsoever things are just, whatsoever things are pure, whatsoever things are lovely, whatsoever things are of good report; if there be any virtue, and if there be any praise, think on these things . . . and the God of peace shall be with you (Philippians 4:6-9).

I diligently complied. Instead of fretting about Raul and fantasizing about Fernando, I started making all my requests known to God. Daily I asked Him to come into Raul's heart, to change him, to make me love him, to protect the boys, to get me a raise, to make my boss like me, to help me at my job, and on and on.

Many times I fell asleep on the bathroom floor, my face buried in my Bible. I memorized whole chapters of Scripture, attempting to brainwash myself with concepts that were true, honest, just, pure, lovely, and of good report. Peace embraced me as the words of God caressed my soul.

I learned that His Word was actually called the Sword. The Sword was fighting for me with its two sharp edges. It was causing me to differentiate between my soul and my spirit. My soul was the center of my will, intellect, and emotions. My spirit could be recognized by its intuition, conscience, and communion with God. Skillfully God's Word was cutting between my joints and marrow, discerning my thoughts and the intentions of my heart.

Whenever I could, I listened to worship music or Bible studies on the radio in order to drown out any thoughts of my past or present circumstances. Soon more Scriptures touched me.

"The wicked, through the pride of his countenance, will not seek after God: God is not in all his thoughts."

(Psalm 10:4). Ouch! That one hurt. I had never thought of myself as wicked of proud. Yet, hadn't I behaved as if I didn't need God or His counsel?

"The fool hath said in his heart there is no God" (Psalm 53:1). Not to believe in God was foolish, leading to an unprofitable life. That wasn't for me! I wanted all that God had for me.

"Let the wicked forsake his way, and the unrighteous man his thoughts: and let him return unto the Lord, and he will have mercy upon him . . . for he will abundantly pardon" (Isaiah 55:7). I had already made the choice to turn from my own thoughts and to seek His. I knew that He had pardoned me—Christ's mission to this earth had been solely to wash my sins and guilt with the blood He shed on Mount Calvary. It was essential that I forsake my thoughts and ways for they were the complete opposite of God's.

"For my thoughts are not your thoughts, neither are your ways my ways, saith the Lord. For as the heavens are higher than the earth, so are my ways higher than your ways, and my thoughts than your thoughts" (Isaiah 55:8,9). Oh, how I longed to think the thoughts of God— to have the mind of Christ!

As I sought to do so, I made another glorious discovery, a single verse of Scripture that was destined to transform my world forever. I found words that no human could ever speak to me—neither Raul, nor Fernado, nor any other mortal could offer me such a promise. Today these words continue to lighten my load, to illuminate my darkness, to guide me through every circumstance:

> For I know the thoughts that I think toward you, saith the Lord, thoughts of peace, and not of evil, to give you an expected end [that for which you are longing] (Jeremiah 29:11).

Imagine—God thinking about me! What an incredible truth! Not only is He thinking about me, He is finding a way to give me the desires of my heart, to fulfill the longings that He put there in the first place!

It wasn't long before I had totally redecorated my house. I planted tulips along the sides of the ugly asphalt walkway, and set camellias under every window in the front of the house—just like at Daddy's. A couple of nights each week I took the boys to the kung fu studio to help Raul work. To my delight, he really seemed to love having us there.

My boss even changed his attitude toward me. Instead of throwing papers on my desk and constantly reprimanding me in front of everyone, he gave me a considerable raise. He also entrusted me with greater responsibilities. His wife and family, who worked with me, treated me with care and kindness. They had no idea about the brutality I still suffered at home on a regular basis. Because of God's favor, they had learned to trust me, to depend on me. Their friendship meant more to me than they will ever know.

God is so good! It was evident that He was working out a plan for my life, even though I had no clue what it could be. I just determined that I would trust Him like a child because His promises were now directing my life.

Now that Raul saw me experiencing peace, he became more uneasy. His anger over my loyal church attendance and my dedication to Bible reading intensified dramatically. As far as I was concerned, I wasn't a "religious freak," as he called me. The fact was, I hated the fanaticism that brought shame to the church; the hypocrisy and the ignorance of God's Word in professing believers. A yearning for the truth is what drew me into having a personal relationship with the One who calls Himself the Truth. I worshiped and studied because I needed to, but that's not the way he saw it.

Raul's mistreatment of me intensified and grew more frequent. He'd grab my face, squeezing his fingers against my eyes or throat. He would kick me in bed, sometimes hurling me onto the floor.

One time he even tried to run me over with his car. It was on a Saturday. Raul seemed very tender toward the boys and decided to spend the day with us. We all jumped into the car and the boys started informing Raul excitedly what each wanted to do. Before long, he and the boys were all arguing about how each of them wanted to spend their fun day. Raul then started shoving the boys around, and I quickly jumped out of the car with them. It was then that he tried to run us over. The boys and I walked home examining bugs, clouds, and any other of God's creations we ran into. We made a picnic when we got home and went to the nearby canyon to enjoy it. Raul didn't come home till late. No matter what He did, God always kept me from getting hurt. I was comforted daily through the Psalms. "It is good for me that I have been afflicted; that I might learn thy statutes" (Psalm 119:71). Suffering had driven me to be in love with God's Word, and that was the most wonderful thing that had ever happened to me.

What disturbed me the most was Raul's inability to love me, or to love anyone else, for that matter. Nor was he able to receive love. I grieved, unable to be comforted, because my husband, the one I had chosen to be my lover and partner for life, might never love me. Even though I knew that God had a plan for me, I was heartsick over the incidents that occurred, leaving me frightened and shaken.

After a year of serious consideration, combined with a sincere dependence upon the Scriptures for guidance, I decided to get out of Raul's life. I had a God-given responsibility to teach the boys God's ways. Raul's uncontrollable anger would eventually damage them, since they were witnessing more of his outbursts with every passing day. Eventually they would learn to abuse their own children and wives.

I had received a couple of phone calls from girls who were looking for Raul. One had expressed shock when I told her that I was his wife. There were occasional nights Raul never came home at all.

According to God's Word, he had broken his marriage vows to me, and before God I believed I was free to leave him. By that time, I wasn't interested in finding another man, and was persuaded that I should guard myself against divorce. I simply hoped that if Raul lost everything he had, he might turn to God the way I had.

It was time for me to prepare to leave him. At that time Shirley lived on the forested campus of a Bible college in Santa Cruz. I had decided that the boys and I would join her there as soon as I could work out all the details.

I had discussed leaving with Raul on several occasions. I was convinced that he didn't believe me. I've since learned that he did. To pamper me into staying he bought me a car. I felt guilty, but I took it. Separation was not what I wanted, but was a step I had to take—one last desperate attempt to save our marriage.

What I really wanted was for Raul to love me enough to not hurt me or the boys anymore. I wanted to be passionately in love with him again, and to have him woo me back to himself.

After five painful years of trying to make my marriage work, I realized I was not able to do it. If Raul were on his own, maybe he would turn to the Lord. There were several Bibles throughout the house, and he knew how to reach God if he needed to call on Him.

I had peace in my heart and a little flicker of excitement about what God was going to do. Maybe now I could be a missionary, a vagabond for Jesus, traveling the seas of the world.

I could do it! I had learned to swim against the world's current. I had defeated the personal emptiness that causes men to drift downstream and into oblivion. In my weakness I had been made strong.

A drastic change was about to occur! But to my amazement, this time the transformation happened in Raul's life, not in mine.

Docked

10

Raul was loudly knocking at the front door. I heard his voice, yelling for me to let him in the house. He never carried a house key, a small annoyance I had long since learned to ignore.

Just a few minutes before, I had walked in the door myself after a Sunday evening Bible study. Before the boys and I had left the church, the pastor had invited people to the altar to make a commitment to God. I had caught a glimpse of Raul rushing in from outside, making his way to the altar for prayer.

I had grabbed the boys' hands and run to the car. I didn't even want to know what he was up to. Raul probably wanted me to see him go up and perform some religious act so I would change my mind about leaving him. He had done this sort of thing before on several occasions. He had also been unsuccessfully exploring Oriental religions in his search for inner peace. I wasn't about to be impressed in the least.

What had impressed me was the sermon I had just heard. It had been health to my bones and strength to my flesh. I wanted to rush home to think about it.

The boys, now three and four, snuggled into the back-seat of my car. As I drove toward the house, I pleaded with God to captivate my thoughts, shielding me from Raul and his nonsense. "Seize my mind with this evening's message," I prayed, and then repeated a Scripture that I knew so well. It had been the pastor's closing verse:

> And God shall wipe away tears from their eyes; and there shall be no more death, neither sorrow, nor crying, neither shall there be any more pain: for the former things are passed away (Revelation 21:4).

The message had concerned the imminent Second Coming of Jesus to establish a new heaven and a new earth. As the pastor spoke, I tried to imagine a day without pain and tears. The idea that God would some-day wipe away all my tears was beyond my comprehension.

But then, knowing Jesus, I could imagine Him doing it! He had always been moved with compassion for those who suffered. Jesus always went out of His way to gently restore a person to spiritual as well as physical whole-ness. He cared for them no matter what their intellectual capacity, social standing, or knowledge of Him. Yes, Jesus could wipe away my tears. He was big enough to become small—just for me. How I longed for Him!

These thoughts restored my hope, a characteristic that had once been dominant in my personality. Hope is not a wishful feeling about the future, nor adherence to some fantasy. It is a God-given virtue which flows into a man's being, stabilizing him, making him confident and filled with expectancy. The Bible says that hope is the anchor of the soul.

Now my own tears were silent prayers which I offered to God. Only He understood the meaning of each one, and I was sure that He stored my tears in His bottles in heaven, just as He did with King David's.

It was in this frame of mind that I drove home. Once the boys were asleep, I had a few more minutes to treasure these assurances. Then Raul had come knocking at our door.

"Sharon! Sharon I'm not mad. I'm not going to hurt you. Open the door, I have to tell you something really neat!"

Maybe he'd clinched a part on some kung fu TV show. There was always something exciting happening in Raul's life, usually involving his studio or his weekend escapes.

I opened the door slightly, not knowing what to expect, and found myself looking directly into Raul's radiant smile. It stretched from ear to ear.

"I'm born again!" he exclaimed. I slammed the door in his face.

Wasn't it a bit blasphemous to claim a "born-again" experience just to impress me? He knew what it meant— we had talked about it enough. Sometimes when he left the notes with the roses, expressing his regrets, I would explain to him that it was impossible for him to change apart from Jesus Christ.

"Sharon . . . open the door . . . please," he pleaded softly. There was a genuine tenderness in his voice I had never heard before. For some reason, it reminded me of the quality I heard when Jesus spoke to my heart—when He pleaded with me to listen to Him. Cautiously, I opened the door. Raul reached for me gently, and held my face between his hands—those same two hands that he had often used to hurt me. He kissed me repeatedly.

"I love you, Sharon. I'm so sorry for everything I've ever done to hurt you. I just want to be a loving husband. Can't we start over? I'll never hurt you again." His words were full of hope and joy. Was I supposed to believe him this time?

"Start over?" I was thinking of my own plans to start over without him.

"I know you don't believe me," his voice was persuasive, "and I understand that. But you'll see. Just give me some time to show you."

"Raul, I'm sorry if I'm not excited, but we've gone through these promises before. And, to tell you the truth, I've been pretty excited about the future I've been planning for myself and the boys." I was actually feeling rather guilty.

He attempted to grab me excitedly as if nothing had ever happened between us. I pushed him away.

"Please! Don't do that. Don't touch me." My voice sounded hard, and I pushed his hands away coldly. I didn't like them near me; they'd hurt me too often. It would be a long time before I would surrender to his advances. No matter how I reasoned with myself, every time he got near me, my flesh froze.

Instantly our roles had changed—now he was the good guy and I was the bad guy. He pursued me and I backed off. Raul wanted me, and he told me that he'd wait forever until I was ready to receive his love. He was talking like Christ talks to His bride, the church, and he'd never even read the Bible.

We sat down and talked. It took us half the night to discuss how it all had happened. He confessed that he couldn't live with himself, realizing fully what he had been doing to the boys and me. He didn't tell me that night, but years later he confessed that he had come home that Sunday evening with the intention of killing all of us. In his desperation, he'd been flicking through all the television channels to pass the time while we were in church. Suddenly he'd been captivated by a gentle man speaking to a group of teenagers about the love of God.

Raul explained the man's message. "He talked about the love of God . . . about His character. He said that God loved me and was the only One that could wash my slate clean and give me a new life. Can you believe it, Sharon?

I'm a new person! I can tell!'' My husband spoke to me as
if he had just discovered a mystery; as if he had been
blind but now could see.

We found out later that the man on the television had
been Chuck Smith. Today we know him as a man who is
absolutely fascinated with the character of God and with
the in-depth teachings of His Word. Pastor Chuck abhors
the fanaticism and emotionalism that's in the church
hindering God's truth from being revealed in its original
simplicity. Although he is a theologian, he is most of all a
marvelous communicator of the unmeasurable love of
God and the way He lavishes it on His people.

Well, under the circumstances, what could I do? I
decided to stay, at least temporarily, watching Raul
closely to determine if his experience was real. If it
wasn't, it would certainly be the cruelest lie he had ever
told me. On the other hand, a true conversion would
open up incredible avenues for me. In time I would be a
missionary! It had to happen. Wasn't it God's will to give
man the desires of his heart? Hadn't He put them there?

It was immediately evident that Raul was a new person, as evidenced by his new outlook and vision for life,
but it took me a couple of years to be thoroughly convinced of his sincerity. In my lifetime I had seen much
hypocrisy in people who turned to God during desperate situations.

Raul's anger continued to explode sporadically, plagu-
ing my mind with doubts. Nevertheless, time and again
I saw him go for walks where he called on God for help
and guidance. This enabled him to extinguish what
might otherwise have become a recurrence of his blazing
fury.

Raul's life-changing experience demonstrated to me
what Christian conversion really is. When a person is
truly born again, he receives forgiveness for his sins and
senses a deep sprirtual cleansing, which produces inner
joy. Aware of the wickedness of his heart, he knows that

he did not merit or earn this forgiveness through his own goodness; he accepts by faith that ". . . the blood of Jesus Christ his Son cleanseth us from all [past, present, and future] sin" (1 John 1:7).

A true convert falls in love with Jesus, even though he may know nothing about Him. As he sees his Lord revealed through the Scriptures and in his life, he develops an even greater hunger to become acquainted with His Savior. His gratitude to Christ compels him to tell others about his experience. He yearns for them, too, to receive forgiveness and freedom from their sins.

A new believer grows spiritually as he nails his old nature to the cross with Christ. He no longer chooses to be controlled by his passions, intellect, or will. Instead, through reading and meditating on the Scriptures, he saturates his mind with God's thoughts. In this way he becomes a new man.

As a new Christian encounters life's daily difficulties, his old nature will try to recapture him. His flesh, with its insatiable cravings, will seduce him. The world, with its false hopes, will lure him, and Satan, the deceiver of mankind, will harass him mercilessly in a mighty attempt to possess his soul.

But, because the convert is becoming acquainted with God through His Word and intimate communion with Him, he learns a new way of thinking—God's way. This strengthens him, and makes him able to resist attacks. In time, the believer is able to surrender to Christ daily, and this transforms him into the image of his God. It takes a lifetime. The Scripture says:

> But we all, with open face beholding as in a
> glass the glory of the Lord, are changed into
> the same image from glory to glory even as by
> the Spirit of the Lord (2 Corinthians 3:18).

Raul's conversion was real. He was miraculously transformed. He was a new creature, a new creation, born again. An incredible metamorphosis had taken place. What a privilege it was to be in the midst of the miracle!

Raul called all of his friends. He cried as he talked to them over the phone, explaining to each one what had taken place. He called my sister Shirley, then his parents, then mine, then his kung fu students, and lastly his old high school buddies.

After giving his kung fu lessons, he presented to his students the biblical truths he was devouring every day. It wasn't long before we had a weekly Bible study meeting at our house, and its number included his friends and students whose lives had already been changed by Raul's witness. Sometimes we stayed up all night praying together until the breaking dawn reminded us to have breakfast.

Although I still felt a personal coldness toward Raul, I could see that he was truly walking with God. He had been loved and forgiven by Jesus; the spiritual understanding of this fact generated a gradual change in all his attitudes. His true repentance was evident. He started taking on more responsibilities around the house and spending his days off with us. It was so, so good—I can still savor it. I was convinced that in time Raul's undisciplined character would be Spirit-controlled. It would probably take forever; that's how it is for all of us. He hadn't become perfect. I would soon see that I hadn't, either.

Our weekly home Bible study grew so big that we were forced to move it to the kung fu studio. By now I had quit my job, so the boys and I would rush over to the studio after Raul's classes were over. We ran the sweeper, sprayed with disinfectant, cleaned the bathroom, watered the plants, and did whatever else we could do to prepare for the study. Later, while Raul taught, I told the kids Bible stories and songs, we danced, and did whatever else it took to keep them entertained. I knew my role well and I loved it.

On Sundays we attended Sunday school and church together, and sometimes we drove to Costa Mesa where Pastor Chuck Smith held Bible studies under a great big tent. Thousands of teenagers and young adults gathered there, learning to understand and obey God's revelation to man.

Those days fulfilled all that my heart yearned for— to spend time with my husband, to work with him, to listen to Bible studies as a family, to pray together, to share our spiritual experiences.

At long last, I began to be infatuated with Raul again. Soon I was wildly in love with him, and wanted to be beside him constantly. Enjoying Raul became my obsession. I didn't seem to need Christ's fellowship that much when Raul and I were in such a close relationship. To this day that intense desire for his attention and company interferes with my communion with God.

I guess that's why Paul made such a specific observation about women and their relationship with Christ:

> The unmarried woman careth for the things
> of the Lord, that she may be holy both in body
> and in spirit: but she that is married careth for
> the things of the world, how she may please
> her husband (1 Corinthians 7:34).

God's Word tells us that God is jealous of relationships that draw us away from Him. It also teaches that one of God's many names is "Jealous." God's jealousy is not like our vicious attitude that stems from pride and rises up from uncontrolled covetousness. His jealousy does not express itself in envy, malice, and hatred.

God's jealousy is manifested in His zeal to protect His relationship with His bride. It is God's jealousy that will not allow us to wander away from His love. Although He fills our hearts with devotion for our loved ones, He will fight to be the Master Lover, and it is only through Him that we are able to love one another with a pure heart.

The apostle Paul expressed this same jealousy when he was concerned that Satan might beguile the church through his subtleties. Paul knew what Satan had done to Eve, and did not want to see him corrupt our minds:

> I am jealous over you with a godly jealousy:
> for I have espoused you to one husband [Jesus]
> that I may present you as a chaste virgin to
> Christ (2 Corinthians 11:2).

It is for this reason that the Lord has not allowed me to be enveloped in Raul. Instead His will draws Raul away from me, forcing me to seek out the true Lover of my soul. He wants me to love Him as wholeheartedly as Raul does.

Raul's passion for Christ attracted him to the Word as well as to the spiritually dying people of the world. He was not satisfied with the conversion of the 200 or 300 people who now attended our weekly studies. He had and still has—an intense drive to share what God has done for him with the entire world. This totally excited me. I could sniff the mission field right around the corner!

He started visiting our high school campus during the students' lunch hour, and talked to them about Jesus. He did the same at other schools. Sharing Christ at kung fu exhibitions became commonplace. I accompanied him as often as I could.

Raul's thirst for the knowledge of God was never quenched. He devoured study books and Pastor Chuck's teaching tapes by the dozens. He attended a special class for men like himself whose passion for the Word consumed them.

Although Raul was making thousands of dollars in his kung fu business, neither the money nor his evident success could compete with his love for God. After about a year of working closely together, I began to notice that Raul was gone more and more, off to one place or another sharing the Good News about Jesus. It was impossible for me to go with him because I had my home and children to care for. I started feeling very lonely again.

One day I sprained my ankle. I asked Raul to stay home from a friend's prayer meeting so he could help me with the boys. Putting them to bed was a long process of storytelling, talking, snacks, drinks of water, and anything else they could think of to get to stay up an extra five minutes. I was shocked when Raul said, "I'm sorry, dear, but you're just going to have to handle this one by yourself. I can't miss the prayer meeting."

Self-pity immediately gripped me. Yes, I knew that prayer was a priority, but didn't he understand? I had been alone so long. Now that he was a Christian, I expected him to be there for me.

My dad had always been gone when I was a child. I barely knew him when we came to the United States to live. And, hidden in a secret closet of my heart, there is a portrait of my mother which never fails to hurt me. I can still see her sitting on her bed alone, early in the morning and late at night, her Bible on her lap and tears rolling down her cheeks. She never knew I saw her that way.

Mother had always been our companion, teaching, loving, and caring for Shirley and me. She was known for her jovial, free spirit and her air of personal contentment. She sang and played the piano for Bible studies, ran our day school and sometimes taught at our evening Bible classes. She counseled, gave music lessons, and always had extra time for a mountain or beach outing. Yet, in spite of her love of life, I never forgot my mother's moments of hidden loneliness. As a child I had determined that my husband would never leave me. Yet now I realized that I had lost my own groom to his new Lord.

I crawled around the house that evening, crying as I went, my ankle throbbing. After a few hours I felt I couldn't handle the pain anymore. I called Raul. Did he feel any guilt? He didn't. Instead he prayed for me.

I felt depression come on like a torrential flood. But, by now, I knew what to do. I looked up all the Scriptures I could think of that had to do with wives, husbands, and the biblical duties of married couples. If Raul was doing God's will, I would learn to love it. As usual, the word brought me to repentance:

> But this I say, brethren, the time is short: it remaineth, that both they that have wives be as though they had none; and they that weep, as though they wept not . . . (1 Corinthians 7:29,30).

Another verse I read instructed believers to walk circumspectly, not as fools, but wisely, redeeming the time because the days are evil. It said that we should seek to understand the will of the Lord.

I was humiliated. People were dying and going to hell, and I was worried about my ankle! Wasn't it about time for me to stop my pity parties and get involved? If I was ever going to be a missionary, I needed to prepare myself.

When I confessed all this to Raul, he was excited. He agreed that I should organize a meeting for women who were interested in sewing quilts and other necessary articles for the mission field. To my disappointment, however, when the meeting day arrived, no one showed up.

I tried everything. But no matter how I searched for just the right activity, I found it was neither pleasing Raul nor attracting a single living soul.

The only people that wanted me were the little children. I loved them too, but for a while I was the only babysitter. We didn't want to ask the new converts to

babysit. During that time I never got to listen to Raul's
Bible studies or to mingle with the adults. In utter bewil-
derment I cried out to God again.

I'll never forget that night. The moon was bright, and
stars twinkled in the clear sky. Sitting on Grandma's
hand-me-down couch gave me a good view of the trees
in our backyard. I usually pray looking out a window.
That night I noticed that our apricot tree was full of
leaves and new fruit, while the neighbors' shade tree
had no leaves at all.

"Raul is the apricot; you're the barren one."

These were the words that came into my mind. And I
had a good idea who had put those thoughts there. God!
I would have never thought of myself as barren. I kept a
clean house, adored my children, and faithfully taught
them the Word. Reading the Word was as much a part of
my daily routine as brushing my teeth.

"Why am I barren?"

I asked the One who knew the intimate secrets of my
heart. And all at once I understood. "You only read the
Bible to find answers to your problems and to ask for
things. You never study just to know Me. You don't tell
anyone about Me. You are content to live a very private
life."

Of course it's appropriate to ask God for things. Christ
instructed us to ask, and promised to give us anything
we request according to His will. What's not pleasing to
Him is when all we do is ask, and when we ask only
according to our own self-centered will.

It was time for me to discover who God is. It was vital
for me to love Him simply for who He is, not for what I
could get out of Him. I needed to ask Him what He
wanted from me and how to accomplish it.

Then the awful truth dawned on me—the reason I had
wanted to get involved in missions wasn't because I
wanted to please Jesus. It wasn't even because I wanted
to help people find God. I wanted to see my missionary

fantasies come true! Now that I thought about it, I had never asked Him what He thought about my plans. I hadn't even asked Him to help me work them out. As I faced the fact that I had nothing of any value to share with anyone, I wept.

No wonder I was docked, stuck at home alone. I remembered a big old ship I once saw in the Valparaiso harbor. It was on a dry dock where seagoing vessels are elevated for repair and reconstruction. This ship had been battered and torn by years of transatlantic voyages. At least ten colors of paint were visible on its severely chipped surfaces. The ship's name was so weatherworn that it could not be read. I remember feeling sorry for it, wondering how many tales it could relate if it could speak. One thing was obvious: It wasn't going anywhere—not now, and not for a long time. Neither was I.

Then another picture came into my mind, one more memory which helped me understand what God was trying to say. Once, when the boys and I built their tree house, I had hammered a bunch of great big nails into the apricot tree. Later on, a gardener told me that the iron would feed the tree, and cause it to produce bigger and better fruit. I wasn't sure if there was any scientific basis for his statement, but it seemed to have been proven true. Once the nails were there, our tree produced multiplied dozens of juicy apricots—more than it had ever yielded before.

Nails—nails to produce fruitfulness . . . Nails had hung Jesus to the rugged Calvary tree. His death had brought forth His resurrection, and had made abundant life available for all who would believe.

Raul had died to his old ways. He had nailed his past to the cross of Jesus, and now was truly alive in the Spirit of God. Meanwhile, I wasn't thinking of the One I was supposed to be loving with all my heart, my soul, and my mind. I was thinking of myself.

I wasn't looking forward to heaven, to an eternity shared with my Maker, the Lover of my soul. I was looking forward to having my personal desires fulfilled during my earthly lifetime. By continuing that outlook, I would miss all that God had for me.

I was trying to save my own life, to live it my own way. Now, in order to find true life, I had to die, too. That's all there was to it.

The Master Shipbuilder

11

Like the old steamer in Valparaiso, my ship needed to be restored for the voyages ahead. Only God could make it fit to carry me to life's various ports and to battle the ocean's storms. I would have to die to my ways and submit to His ways, His will, and the skillfulness of His hands. I could not repair myself.

I must have heard the words a thousand times: "I am crucified with Christ, nevertheless I live." Now I was about to learn their meaning, personally and practically.

We "die to ourselves" when we decide that our human will can only make us barren, and therefore unhappy.

We "die" when we realize that God's plans and purposes for us are the only viable ones and must be brought about in His way, in His time.

We "die" to this lifetime when we turn our eyes toward eternity and cease to live for earthly satisfaction.

"Barren" is a very desolate word. It means unproductive, unfruitful, and sterile. Jesus taught that a vine which doesn't produce fruit is cut off, withers, and is then thrown into the fire.

He also said that if a branch is purged and cut back it will bring forth much fruit. I had been in the church all

my life, growing like a wild weed, doing whatever I
pleased. Now creation's Husbandman wanted to purge
me. He began to cut off my dead branches so I could
produce something useful, even sweet. I wondered what
it would be.

I looked up the word "barren" in my Bible concordance. I found a Scripture written to the bride of Christ,
the church. This passage, found in the Book of Isaiah,
became the foundation upon which I was to build the
remaining years of my life:

> Sing, O barren, thou that didst not bear;
> break forth into singing, and cry aloud, thou
> that didst not travail with child: for more are
> the children of the desolate than the children of
> the married wife, saith the Lord (Isaiah 54:1).

The Lord was calling me to rejoice. He wanted me to
realize a great truth: A desolate (or in my case, lonely)
woman can be more spiritually fruitful than a woman
whose life is absorbed only by her husband and her
natural children.

"Enlarge the place of thy tent," the Scripture continued, "and let them stretch forth the curtains of thine
habitations: spare not, lengthen thy cords, and strengthen
thy stakes." In more simple words, Make room! Open your
house and stretch your heart. Be strengthened in the Lord.

"For thou shalt break forth on the right hand and on
the left." God made it clear to me that He had a plan for
fruitfulness in my life. And, private as I had become
since my high school days, the thought of this frightened me a little.

"Fear not; for thou shalt not be ashamed: neither be
thou confounded; for thou shalt not be put to shame: for
thou shalt forget the shame of thy youth . . . " I had been
ashamed of my premarital pregnancy and my sick marriage. I suffered reproach over the horrible things Raul

had once said to me. His words had wounded me, leaving scars that refused to be healed. Had God forgiven and forgotten? Then so should I.

". . . and shalt not remember the reproach of thy widowhood any more. For thy Maker is thine husband; the Lord of hosts is His name. . . ." The concept was new, revolutionary, and absolutely breathtaking! My Maker, the Lord of all creation, is my Husband! On my wedding day I had verbally said my vows to God. It was time for me to start living them.

Now the picture became even more clear. Even though I was married to Raul, the studio and the ministry occupied from five to six days and evenings a week. I was a widow—a widow chosen by God. He would care for me as my Husband. He was calling me to cleave to Him, to depend upon Him. I was to lean on Him for support and to draw my nourishment from Him alone.

At first I was elated. But then, as always, the glories of God's truth were soon overshadowed by my day-to-day life. Baseball games, loud drums, street hockey, Boy Scouts, unlovable pets, school outings, chauffeuring kids, dentist appointments, complaining neighbors, model building, bug collecting, stream fishing, boxing matches, and other unfeminine distractions made God's concepts seem distant and impractical.

How I missed my sister! And since Raul's conversion, Chrissy was no longer allowed to come to our house, so I missed her too. I only saw Aunt Phene once or twice a year. My South American childhood still affected me in that I felt out of place. It was still hard for me to relate to American people in an intimate way so I remained more or less friendless. I believe I chose not to establish roots in America so I would not be hurt as deeply as I had been when I left Chile. Inspired as I had been by God's Word, it wasn't long before loneliness began to taunt me.

One day a huge ten-year old boy came knocking on my front door.

"Hi, my name is Tony."

"Hi, what can I help you with?" I barely opened the door. "Can I come in?"

"No, I don't think so. What do you want?"

"Aren't you Raulie and Shane's mom?"

"Yes."

"Well, then why can't I come in?" he questioned insistently and stuck his big foot in my front door so I couldn't close it.

"I think you better go right now!" I said sternly.

"No!" he persisted.

"What on earth do you want?"

He removed his foot, looked down and sadly said, "Oh . . . nothing" as he walked away.

"Suffer [let, allow] little children to come unto me and forbid them not: for of such is the kingdom of God." I could hear Christ's words commanding me, burning in my heart.

"He's not little!" I pointed out to God. There was a moment of deafening silence.

"Hey, Tony!" I ran out to the street. Tony played hard-to-get.

"Whaddaya want?" he yelled in disgust.

"Come back later and I'll tell you some Bible stories."

Tony's face lit up with a smile. He came back 30 minutes later, bringing the entire neighborhood with him. Tony worked energetically to set up a huge classroom in the garage. Later on it was moved into our house.

Raulie, Shane, and I would put on puppet shows and plays. We would dance, sing, and plan contests and exciting outings for all the children. By the time my sons started school, it wasn't unusual to share our breakfast and devotion time with six or eight boys who would stop to pick them up on their way to school. It bothered my boys if their friends didn't know Jesus, so they would tell them about Him as soon as the could. Most of the children gave their lives to Christ and are still in love with Him today.

For years Tony nearly drove me to insanity, insisting that I teach him anything and everything I knew. He squeezed out every ounce of patience I had ever had, and drove me to plead with God for more. Mercilessly, he chipped away at my accumulated layers of old paint.

During the years that I was docked, Tony was my constant companion. Since then hundreds of my sons' friends have been welcome in my house, giving me plenty of excuses to repaint, remodel, and redecorate. Just as the Scripture had taught me, with God's help I have "... enlarged ... stretched forth ... spared not ... lengthened and strengthened" not only my tent, and my heart, but also the hearts of my children.

In the meantime, Raul's Bible study was still growing dramatically and was demanding his constant attention. By then we were having double sessions in the kung fu studio and renting buildings for the kids. Raul had a group of faithful men working with him, so there wasn't as much for me to do there. It was at this time that Debbie and Steve entered our lives. Debbie and I soon discovered that God had revealed to each of us His role as our Husband. Some years later Debbie would show me, as no one else could, how our "marriages" with Him only begin on this earth, and soon will lead us all into his wonderful presence forever.

Raul continued to be gone day and night, teaching Bible studies, visiting schools, studying, and doing kung fu exhibitions. We didn't even ride in the same car any more. He left at dawn on Sundays to pray and meditate on the Scriptures. How I missed him.

But God had a message for me even in my yearning for my husband. His absence became another nail, one that gnawed at me every day. Its wound continues to feed my branches.

I still miss Raul on a daily basis. I have never become accustomed to his being gone. And, truthfully, I never want to get used to being without him. I like longing for him. It teaches me self-control. It forces me to die to my desires, and it drives me to Jesus. It's a down-to-earth teaching on how we, the bride of Christ, should yearn for our Lord. Our hearts should be longing painfully for His return.

We live in a day when people are afraid to hurt. We run to and fro, searching for something or someone to relieve the aching inside. Pain cleanses the soul, it adds character to its recipient. If we do not suffer, we cannot receive the depth of God's comfort. If we have not been wounded, we have not felt the tender touch of the Healer. If we have not been alone, we have really not understood the sweetness of His constant companionship. Pain writes the songs and teaches the lessons by which man is comforted. My necessary separation from Raul has birthed in me a longing for heaven, where there is no loneliness or pain.

One evening Raul burst through the door, bringing some totally exciting news. "A couple of the guys and I are going to go to Chile to 'spy out the land.' We want to see about doing some missionary work there." Joshua had done the same thing before the Hebrew children entered the Promised Land to possess it. Was my Promised Land coming into sight, too?

"When are we leaving?"

"I'm sorry, Sharon, but you can't go."

"I can't go? Why?"

"This is ministry, Sharon. Women can't go along."

I had been involved in ministry all my life. Never once had I felt that I was not a part of my dad's ministry. Our family had always been "the Farrels, who are missionaries."

But, much to my amazement, I heard a self-controlled Sharon say, "You'll love Chile. It's wonderful!"

Raul's early experience in the ministry only involved
working with men. At that time, he assumed that this
was the proper way. Later, as he looked deeper into the
Scriptures, he learned that Jesus and the apostles were
surrounded with women who ministered to their needs
and to the needs of others. Paul called them his co-workers
and fellow servants. Jesus honored devout women in an
even more significant way. He allowed them to be the
last to see Him on the cross, and to be the first to see Him
alive again. A woman was the earliest one to proclaim
the good news of the resurrection!

Raul left for Bible study and I flopped onto Grandma's
couch. "Snip, snip!" I could hear heaven's pruning
shears cutting at my dead branches of unbelief, pride,
and anxiety.

"Not yet," the Gardener whispered to my heart.

I became angry, with a talking-through-my-teeth kind
of anger.

It's okay to question God. Just don't sin against Him or
accuse Him falsely while you're blowing off hot air.

"Why can't I go?" I confronted Him. "You know I've
always wanted to go to Chile. I've been waiting for 13
long years!" As if He didn't remember.

"Is it fair that I'm home with all the work, the boys,
and everything else? Is it fair that I babysit all the kids at
church and don't get to do the things I want to do! Raul is
gone all the time. I'm sick of doing it all alone." My
angry flesh exploded, and then I fell silent.

I decided now that I'd said my piece, I'd best be quiet
and listen. I really didn't expect an answer—not after
that emotional outburst. I didn't even open my Bible for
once. I closed my eyes in silence.

In my mind's eye, I pictured an immensely large,
strong ox. Its muscles were bulging with power.

"That's you," said an inner voice.

"Thanks, I always wanted to be an ox."

Then a Scripture came into my mind:

Take my yoke upon you, and learn of me; for I am meek [power under control] and lowly [humble] in heart: and ye shall find rest unto your souls. For my yoke is easy, and my burden is light (Matthew 11:29,30).

I understood that I was to put on Christ's yoke—that was His will for me. I needed to learn the way our Servant God leads us in His service. I was to submit in unquestioning obedience to the One who controls the existence of everything. He would give my anxious heart rest.

I also perceived that the ox is the symbol of servant-hood in the Bible. God was calling me to be a willing servant.

I then pictured this ox pulling a very small cart bearing my two rambunctious little boys. The ox's neck was uncomfortably enclosed in an enormous two-oxen yoke which was leaning awkwardly toward one side. One ox was clearly missing, and if he had been there he would have held the yoke in balance. I was trying to bear a yoke made for two oxen by myself.

I knew who the missing party was, of course. It was Raul. My life without him seemed unbalanced—it rubbed, it put too much weight on my shoulders. I had worn myself out complaining about it.

"Is that fair?" I asked God as I visualized the scene.

Then I pictured Him, the Just One who bore the cruelty of the cross. With His nail-scarred hand, He picked up the yoke on the empty side and held it just right, releasing the pressure from the ox. He bore the burden Himself.

"What if I lighten your load?" a soft voice whispered to my heart. I felt a tremendous surge of joy and understanding.

"Anytime, my Lord" was my ardent reply.

Little by little, I was developing a keen sense of hearing.

God was speaking through His Word to my conscience. Chipping away the paint from my landlocked ship was a difficult chore, but it felt so healthy, so wonderful. I was beginning to feel brand-new and ready to sail. All I needed was a destination!

Raul was deeply moved by my newly developing relationship with Christ. He asked me to communicate what God had done for me with the women in our church. Perhaps I might even start a women's study. I was a private person, remember? I didn't like telling people about my past life. It was buried and that was that. Besides, how could I handle a women's study. What would I do with a bunch of American women anyway? I had already failed once when I had tried to get women together to sew items for the mission field. That was enough for me! I turned down the offer without ever asking God.

After a terrible injury suffered during a kung fu exhibition, Raul's brother, Xavier, received the miracle of the indwelling Jesus into his life. When he married a beautiful girl named Trudy, she promptly decided to be my best friend. At first her company bothered me. She came to our home frequently, and I was always busy in my career as a homemaker, mom, neighborhood watchman, and sitter. I really had no time to visit with anyone.

Furthermore, I couldn't relate to her at all. She was young and a very typical American girl. I finally decided that if she was going to hang around, she'd just have to watch me do my stuff.

It didn't bother her a bit. If I sewed, she'd bring her machine over and sew right alongside me. If I cleaned, she would help me. We planted flowers, cooked, shopped; what I did, she did. And, unbelievable as it seems, when I got pregnant, she did too. We have the proof.

Trudy and I became the best of friends. She was a woman that God chose to be my intimate friend. He brought her to the place where I was docked, knowing that she would paint my surfaces bright and sunny colors—all the exotic hues I loved.

Her sense of humor was just what I needed. Because of the adventurous life I had once led, my present life seemed boring. She taught me to joke about the menial duties that chained me. I learned that even imprisonment could be productive.

My thoughts turned toward Joseph, whose story appears in the Book of Genesis. Unjustly sold as a slave by his jealous brothers, Joseph was falsely accused and imprisoned. But he channeled his heartbreaking circumstances into productivity. First, by being a good steward, he received the position of Pharoah's prison warden. Later, when God finally had him released, he was placed second in command to Pharaoh, ruling over the great nation of Egypt.

From his prison cells, the apostle Paul wrote letters of comfort and instruction. His sole transgression was that he was an ardent follower of Jesus Christ and a vagabond missionary of the highest rank. Guilty of following in Jesus' steps, he became an "ambassador in bonds." In his teachings, he relates the Christian walk to prison life, calling himself a "prisoner of the Lord Jesus Christ."

Maybe someday I, too, would write something—a song or a poem that would share how chains of love have held me to His will.

Our church started meeting in a rented theater, holding double sessions of approximately 500 people each. Still it continued to grow. Raul's heart rejoiced with each person that made a decision for Christ. He had only one desire: to declare the love of God to a decaying world.

Although he studied the Word eight hours a day, searching it from cover to cover, his passion for it compelled him to crowd his schedule even more. He enrolled in a Christian university.

I had been taking kung fu lessons so I could spend a little extra time with Raul. I took a beating three nights a

week to be with this guy! I would have preferred to be
wrapped up in a blanket with him in front of the fireplace, kissing and eating popcorn until Jesus came back
and caught us!

Again, God had other plans. I was about to be further
refined by the "little things" in life—things which either
sharpen your character or shred it to pieces.

Raul was in the kitchen having breakfast; Trudy sat
next to him.

"Guess what, my dear?" I couldn't wait to surprise
him. "We're going to have another baby!"

"No! It can't be!" He jumped up excitedly. Raul Jr. was
seven and Shane was six. I'd had two miscarriages in the
past two years, and we'd felt our childbearing days were
over. I have never seen Raul so happy!

How an intelligent human being can call his offspring
a "product of conception," minimizing his humanity in
order to cover his murderous act of abortion, is beyond
my comprehension. There is nothing as exhilarating as
having a baby, especially when you know that God is the
originator of life. The miracle of it, of two becoming one,
leaves the greatest minds baffled.

Trudy was happy for me, but I had learned to read her
mind. She wanted a baby, too! Within four months, she
conceived. We thoroughly enjoyed ourselves getting fat
together and reminiscing about all the perils I had survived with Raulie and Shane.

We named our new son Ryan Brent ("little king").
Along with him came the usual little furniture, little
clothes, little stories, little hurts, little tears, little friends,
little time, little sleep, and mountains of diapers to be
changed, washed, folded, and stacked!

One morning I woke up early. Ryan had been up all
night. The entire house had been set up to accommodate
Raulie and Shane's army battlefield. They had barri-
caded every door with booby traps that fell on my head,
rang bells, or entwined around my legs. Meanwhile, a

dozen unfinished boys' outfits were piled on my sewing machine, the kitchen was its usual mess, Grandma's couch was still warped, and a heap of "smelling fresh" diapers that almost reached my waist lay in the middle of my bedroom floor, defying me to fold them.

I hated the diapers—every single last clean one of them. They looked like an altar where something needed to be sacrificed, like the altars in the Old Testament where our forefathers sacrificed lambs to God.

I knew very well that Christ had become ". . . the Lamb of God, which taketh away the sin of the world." He had offered Himself as the final sacrifice.

There was only one thing that needed to be sacrificed around our house. Me. I had to die—again—to my will. I needed to submit, once and for all, to the life God had called me to live. I lived in America, not on the mission field. I was constantly alone, restricted from Raul's companionship. I was surrounded by children day and night.

"Oh God, help me!" I cried out, as I threw myself on top of the diapers, flat on my back. Then I quoted my dying prayer right out of Romans 12:1, personalizing it to fit my need. I recited it the way Americans pledge the flag.

"I present my body a living sacrifice, holy, and acceptable unto God which is my reasonable service. I will not be conformed to this world but I will be transformed by the renewing of my mind that I may prove what is the good, and acceptable, and perfect will of God. Amen."

That was it. I was totally sick of trying to make God's will happened for me. I needed to kill all my desires for Chile, the Colombian mission on the hill, and everything I had ever dreamed of becoming. I gave the Master Shipbuilder my life completely, to design it, construct it, and finish it as He pleased, ready for the destination of His choice—no questions asked.

"I will be a living sacrifice." (I still thought it would be a bit more exciting to be a martyr out in the jungle somewhere.)

"I will be holy and acceptable." This wasn't because of my good behavior. It was because He'd cleansed me with His blood, and that was sufficient for me!

"Through His renewing of my mind, I will become transformed. I will allow His good, acceptable, and perfect will to bleed through my being."

It wasn't the first time I would have to put my will on an altar. It wouldn't be the last, either. But isn't eternity forever? This life is only the beginning. And, fortunately, that gives the Shipbuilder, my Maker, all the time He needs to prepare me for the voyages of His choosing.

Traveling First-Class

12

The magnificent snowcapped Andes Mountains can be seen from any part of Santiago. As a young girl, I had taken that for granted. Now, at 34, I savored every detail of Chilean life, culture, and scenery. The main walk in the center of the city was lined with vendors. Many displayed the ship-shaped carts I recalled from childhood, black smoke rising from their smokestacks, their "decks" filled with goodies of all sorts. A crowd of people gathered around the organ man as his monkey grasped for pesos, one after another.

Santiago had grown into a modern, dynamic metropolis. I took dozens of pictures of contemporary glass high rises. These contrasted starkly with the older, more ornate buildings and streetlights which stood in European-style splendor, having survived decades of devastating earthquakes and abuse from times of revolution.

It was a warm October evening. The harsh Chilean winter was over, and every citizen of Santiago seemed to be parading in the streets, enjoying the emerging spring. I was outside for my own reasons, absorbing every aspect of the life I had missed for so long. Any moment I expected to wake up out of this exhilarating dream, but I never did. This was real! It was really me walking on the streets of Chile after 21 years of yearning.

A tugging in Raul's heart had first brought us to this country two months before. I had spent much of the two weeks in my hotel room, looking up acquaintances in the telephone book.

I was delighted to locate my little red-haired friend, Francisca (Panchy) Inostrosa—the one who counted while we played hide-and-seek. It took me a while to find her, but I finally did. Jobless and living with her mother, she had also been a victim of life's cruelty. She had lost her nine-year job as an assistant director at the national television station. An actress for six years before that, she was now unemployed and had suffered the blows of two broken marriages. Due to erroneous child-rearing beliefs she had accumulated throughout her life, she and her little son were having a thoroughly miserable time together.

After spending about an hour reminiscing about the old days, laughing hilariously, and taking pictures, she suddenly turned to me and asked the question of a lifetime: "You're different, Sharon. What do I have to do to be happy like you?"

"Be in love with Jesus" was my immediate reply.

I gave her a Bible and told her to start reading in the Book of John. She has since begun to work out life's problems according to God's ways, and she's reaping the benefits.

Today Panchy works with Lindy Mann, one of our church's missionaries in Chile. She answers most of his mail personally, responding to the hundreds of young people who tune in to Lindy's highly popular radio program. Meanwhile, in several orphanages throughout the city, she brings Bible stories alive, teaching young and old alike about the character of God and how He relates to their lives.

After visiting with several other childhood companions on this second trip, at last I found Fernando Leighton, who today is well-known in Chile as a television director, and producer of a very popular talk-show. Like me, he had been deeply wounded by the misfortunes of life. How thankful I was to learn that he was now married to a beautiful woman, the proud father of three gorgeous children. It was so good to see him, to know that he was well and happy.

During our visit, we poured out the past. The moments were intense. I told him about my Husband, my Maker, who had won my heart to Himself. Fernando, too, had been earnestly seeking Him and was convinced that all creation displayed His handiwork.

When I returned two years later, I sensed the peace that only God can give beginning to control his life. By the Lord's grace alone, today we are the kind of dear friends that I always longed for us to be.

This second trip had brought me to Santiago with two of our church staff's personnel. Our intention was to organize a music festival, with the purpose of presenting Jesus to the young Chilean community in a nonreligious format.

Chile, like many countries in the world, is swamped with the kind of artificial religious piety that is not only disgusting in the sight of man, but is an insult to the heart of God. This kind of religiosity oppresses individuals who sincerely seek intellectual understanding. It also stands in the way of a truly spiritual, intimate relationship with our Creator.

The city had closed down for the weekend, so there wasn't much we could do about the "Escape Festival" until Monday. I decided to stroll through the crowds by myself while my friends entertained themselves at a nearby arcade. As I rounded a corner, a strange encounter occurred. I was abruptly stopped by the most handsome man I have ever seen.

His skin was very white, completely unblemished. Soft, jet-black curls crowned his head. He was tall, and perfectly built. I can still see the long black eyelashes that fringed his deep blue eyes. He quickly looked me over from head to toe.

"Hello, most beautiful woman," he spoke seductively.

"Hi." I knew instinctively that I should have ignored him, but I answered automatically. I hadn't seen anything like this in years. I'd been home having babies!

"What are you doing in my country?" His piercing look immobilized me. I noticed different shades of blue blending in his eyes.

"We're here to do a Christian concert and . . ." For a second I thought I would tell him about Jesus, but in the middle of my sentence, I realized that something peculiar was going on. I began to tremble with fear, even though I was perfectly safe, surrounded by hundreds of people and within sight of several policemen.

"I want you," he said confidently, with no hesitation whatsoever.

By now I was panic-stricken. My legs grew weak, feeling as if they might actually collapse under me. I didn't know where to go. I had told my companions I would meet them on that same corner in another hour. I spotted a bench in the middle of the walkway, and told the man I had to go and wait for my friends. I turned my back on him and walked away. He followed me, sitting down close beside me.

"Let's go for a walk. I want to show you something," he said trying to coax me.

I wasn't about to go anywhere with this seducer. Yet I found myself fighting a strong urge to look at him, to study him. Such physical perfection is seldom seen in a man. Inwardly I cried out to the most beautiful of all, the

Lord of lords. The man left and I was rescued.

Later on, I thought of the time when the prince of this world, Satan, had taken Jesus to an "exceeding high mountain." He had shown Him all the kingdoms of the world and offered them to Him, if He would fall down and worship him.

I had seen men approach women before, preying on their emptiness. But never in my life have I felt such evil, luring deception as I sensed in that man. I went to bed that night thinking about a verse of warning: ". . . for Satan himself is transformed [fashions himself] into an angel of light."

As I asked God for His wisdom regarding this incident, He showed me that He was alerting me to the temptations of every kind that lay in my path. He explained that I had been docked to prepare my ship for battle. I could expect the enemy to launch a full-scale battle against me and my endeavors. This didn't frighten me, because I was already becoming keenly aware of the presence of spiritual warfare. I think it's probably the same sensation a soldier feels when he's dropped out of a helicopter into the middle of a firefight.

The apostle Paul instructed us in Ephesians 6:12,13:

> We wrestle not against flesh and blood, but against principalities, against powers, against the rulers of the darkness of this world, against spiritual wickedness in high places. Wherefore take unto you the whole armor of God, that ye may be able to withstand in the evil day.

He has acquainted us with methods for fighting these rulers of darkness. We are to put on God's armor, as described in His Word. Paul graphically compared the Christian's attire to that of a soldier of his day to whom the apostle was probably chained during the time he wrote this portion of Scripture. He certainly would have had a good look at his guard's weapons and attire.

I understood that the pure, simple message of Christ was not welcome in Chile, in America, or anywhere else on earth where Satan is successfully beguiling men to himself. Man, through the lusts of his flesh, willingly sinks into corruption, not recognizing his tempter. The devil certainly knows the bait necessary to lure the weak in spirit into a hideous eternity without God.

How easily man's confidence in his acquired knowledge, financial situation, career, or standing in society causes him to loathe the wisdom of God. The Scripture says that the world by its own wisdom cannot know God. It also asserts that God's foolishness is wiser than man's wisdom, and His weakness stronger than man's might. God promises that He will ultimately make the self-reliant man look foolish.

My encounter with the handsome tempter reminded me that within myself I didn't have the intellectual, spiritual, or physical capacity to withstand the enemy's assault. This was big-time stuff. Unlike the situation at home, we weren't trying to take over a neighborhood for Jesus. We were after an entire country! It was exciting to realize that as different as the circumstances were, however, the biblical principles I had learned at home would serve me well here, too. Power comes from God, through prayer and obedience to His Word.

I knew it worked—it was prayer and obedience that had accomplished one of the greatest victories in our lives.

When God first convicted me about the barrenness of my life, He immediately told me to forgive Raul's family and to reach out to them once again. Even during our estrangement from them, we had continued to pray for them. Now, one by one, the members of the Ries family began to present their hearts to God.

Josie, Raul's mother, had never been able to find inner peace either through religion, family ties, or psychotherapy classes. How we rejoiced when we learned that she had found rest for her soul in Christ.

Papi, Raul's dad, had been a hopeless alcoholic whose addiction had destroyed his liver. One glorious night he was instantly cured both physically and spiritually. Today Josie and Papi are two of the most loving people I know.

Sonia, Xavier, and Chrissy have all presented their lives to God's service and, along with their spouses, each one is involved in Christian ministry. Among us, we have eight children, all of whom are following Jesus. There is not a day I don't thank God for His keeping power and for the gifts He has given our family, unmerited by us.

To be His child is to travel first-class through this life's journey.

My own family also continues to be an endless source of blessing. Shirley is, as ever, my close and faithful friend. Norman, the husband God chose for her, is the fine man that Shirley deserves, and the brother I never had. With him, Raul and I are free to share our deepest feelings. His storytelling and dry humor have kept Raul and me up many a night, hilariously laughing our troubles away. Their children, Normy and Vanessa, are gifts from our Father to all of us.

When my youngest son, Ryan, was five, just before I first returned to Chile, Daddy retired as a schoolteacher, and he and Mother returned to Colombia. Their hearts' desire was to rebuild the mission where "the two rivers meet and defy the terrain." They wanted to start a school in that area—a primitive region which has seen little improvement since the infernal destruction that condemned their vision to death. A short time before they arrived in Colombia, they were asked to take over a church in the big city of Villavicencio which had suffered from the negligence of an uncaring, self-seeking leader. They heeded to the emergency and stayed. As veteran warriors, they battled the opponent and paved the way to what is now a flourishing, respected Bible and education center in that town.

Their deserted mission still languishes on its hill. Many times, in the privacy of my heart, I have rebuilt her walls, mended her wounds, dressed her windows, and decorated her rooms. I've reached out into the nearby jungle, inviting the poor and weary, welcoming them to receive meat for their bodies and strength for their souls. My prayer has been:

> Oh that I might go win them
> Oh that I might sow in them
> Jesus the Lamb,
> Sacrificed for man
> Oh that I might go—
> Send me!

Recent years have found me in Chile and Colombia two or three times a year, co-laboring with our mission-hearted staff. When I stop to consider the way God fulfills man's deepest desires, my spirit bows in adoration to Him.

God has granted me the opportunity to labor side by side with my boys. One time Ryan and I worked with 30 other builders from our church to reconstruct a big house. It had been bought by the "cheerful givers" at our Calvary Chapel in West Covina. Through the exhausting, exciting hours of planning, buying, laboring, and decorating, I was reminded of Jesus' promise in Luke 18:29 to the disciples who had left all to follow Him:

> There is no man that hath left house, or parents, or brethren, or wife, or children, for the kingdom of God's sake, who shall not

receive manifold more in this present time,
and in the world to come life everlasting.

I thought of my sons, who have followed us onto the mission field. Many times they have given up their vacation months for the promise of greater rewards. Today it is evident that they have not suffered! On the contrary, they have been marvelously enriched. Raul and I are grateful to share the love, joy, and excitement that surrounds them. They are our best friends and we are theirs. Now they, too, have an exciting vision to contribute to the world. Better yet, we plan to spend eternity together.

God has given me countless opportunities to cooperate in music outreaches, pastors' conferences, women's retreats, orphanage visits, and communion with those who, like me, are enthralled with Christ. But no matter how many times I've gone to the mission field, my two-to-four-week journey's have never completely satisfied my yearning to remain in "the regions beyond."

Here in this country where we enjoy the means and the freedom of worship, we have our choice of several dozen radio or TV teachers. We can hear what we want, depending on the mood we're in. In some countries there isn't one Bible-teaching radio program.

"Oh Father," I often prayed after returning home from South America, "why should I stay here where there is such an overabundance of Your truth? In Your Word You said to Your Son, 'Ask of Me, and I shall give thee the heathen for thine inheritance, and the uttermost parts of the earth for thy possession!' That's what I'm asking for, Lord—that you may use me to reach the hearts of the heathen in the uttermost parts of the world for You! Is that too much to ask for? If it is, I am sorry."

Time and again I lifted this secret prayer to God. In one sense, my heart had learned contentment. But it continued to throb with passion for those who are unacquainted with Christ's love.

Raul called me from work one day. "Sharon, you won't believe this!"

I probably would believe it, knowing Raul and knowing God.

"Some movie producers want to make a film of my life."

"Incredible! When?"

"They're coming out next week. They want us to record some information about our lives on tape so they can write the script."

"Raul, I'm not telling anybody about my life. That's private! I've never told anyone about my pregnancy. My parents are missionaries and know thousands of people in South America. I don't want to shame them and . . ." I rattled on.

"Well, you'd better talk to God about it because I know it's His will for us. Stop thinking about yourself. Think about the people it will help. I'm going to do it with or without your approval."

I lay flat on the couch, reasoning with myself. If God had cast my sins as far as the east is from the west, remembering them no more, why did the whole world have to know about them? What was the purpose? God was blessing our ministry in a wonderful way. Thousands of people were being fed from the Scriptures. The missionary vision, which had first captivated Raul and me, was spreading throughout our church.

"Father, only if You command it, I will do it in Jesus' Name. But why do I have to be a spectacle for all to see?"

The answer was simple. It came from the heart of Jesus: "I was made a spectacle before all the world. And I was sinless."

Humbled, I contemplated His Words to me. Two thousand years before, Christ had borne His cross, with angry throngs pressing against Him from all around. In the terrible hours that followed, He allowed Himself to be hung between heaven and earth, suffering the reproach and scorn of mankind. Only His angels and those who loved Him stood in silent adoration while the earth trembled and groaned at the insanity and blasphemy of it all. The Creator had allowed Himself to be crushed and put to shame by His own created beings. This is the way He chose to demonstrate the depth of His love for us.

"Yes, Lord." My heart submitted, knowing that it was Christ's obedience to the Father that had brought new life into the decaying heart of mankind. I would obey, too.

In the days to follow, God's purpose for using my life story became more evident to me. In the Book of Revelation, we can read that Satan, the dragon or accuser of the brethren, is overcome by the blood of the Lamb and by the Word of the saints' testimony. I already knew that the blood of the Lamb could cleanse my sins and defend me from Satan. But I had never realized that my testimony is also an overcoming weapon. I became excited about what God would do with it, and how it would affect the heart of man. Christ had become a spectacle to give life to man. Why shouldn't I?

Keenly aware of the way God uses man's testimony, Satan set out to mentally torture me. As our story was written and the movie was filmed, it became extremely difficult for me to relive my past in such a detailed form. Some days I hated Raul for what he had done to me. I wanted him to pay. I fought the strongest urges to leave him that I have ever felt. How wicked my heart can become at times! Thank God, the cross of Jesus stood tall and reminded me daily that He had already paid the penalty for all of our sins—Raul's and mine.

Unless God brings the past to our remembrance for His own eternal purposes, it is not profitable to wallow in past hurts or to dig out that which has been forgiven and forgotten. He can always be trusted to work all things together for good—past, present, and future.

After the film was released, I went to several churches "under cover" to see people's reactions. One night hundreds of people were flowing into a well-known sanctuary in Los Angeles. In a self-protective daze, I joined them to see Sharon become a spectacle to the world. On my way in, a young man asked me, "Have you seen this movie?"

"Yes, I have," I answered, and not a word more.

"It changed my life!" he exclaimed.

I swallowed the lump that swelled in my throat. I sat down next to a large family which virtually bubbled with joy and laughter. One of the teenage girls sitting next to me politely asked, "Have you seen 'Fury to Freedom'?"

"Yes . . . " I barely answered.

"Well, it led our entire family to Jesus, and all my friends' lives have been changed because of it."

"I've experienced some drastic changes too," I agreed with her. That was enough for me. I had to get up and empty the hidden buckets of tears—tears of joy and shame mingled together. Joy, because of the words I had heard, bearing witness to the life-changing power of the film. Shame, because I'd been such a brat, trying to protect myself, as usual. Sometimes I wonder why God never gets sick of me. I do.

After this "soap opera" trauma, I was ready to continue my pursuit of missions. I went back to praying my "heathen, uttermost" prayer. One day while I meditated on this Scripture hoping to glean a profound revelation from it, gentle words crossed my mind.

"I've already given you the heathen and the uttermost parts of the world."

It occurred to me that, through the movie and Raul's book which had also been written, the two of us were about to become missionaries all over the world at the same time! We were going to the far corners of the globe, to small islands as well as vast continents, to prisoners as well as free men. We were in orphanages, churches, on street corners, with government officials, inside police headquarters, in the privacy of living rooms, behind enemy lines, here, there, and everywhere. What a God! He is a Mastermind with a master plan. It was so big I had almost missed it, and yet God had promised it to me all along:

> For I know the thoughts that I think toward you, saith the Lord, thoughts of peace, and not of evil, to give you an expected end [that which you long for] (Jeremiah 29:11).

At about this time, I began to realize that I was passionately in love with Jesus. His love for mankind was my obsession. His words and continuous guidance demonstrated the quality of love He had for me. I had an ardent desire to see Christ as He is, not as man sees Him, but as the Word of God portrays Him. Reading Scripture in this light gives me an even deeper desire to know Jesus as the Lover of my soul, Eternal Companion, and faithful Husband.

And you know what? Raul is never jealous of Him. When my relationship with Christ is thriving, my love for Raul has no bounds. When my fellowship with Jesus is broken, my relationship with Raul suffers, too. Chapter 5 of the Song of Solomon gives a beautiful description of the Christ I long to behold:

> What is thy beloved [Jesus] more than another beloved, O thou fairest among women [the bride]? What is thy beloved [Jesus] more than another beloved [anything or anyone we love more than Christ]. . . . My beloved is white [pure] and ruddy, the chiefest among ten thousand.

Now long ago, my caring Husband led me to Colombia with a group from our church. Our plan was to take the movie there, once it was completed.

Before leaving on our journey, we discussed some recent kidnappings, as well as the various other perils we might well encounter in the course of our travels. We encouraged ourselves as a group to willingly present our bodies as a sacrifice unto God if such a choice were to be made. This was easier said than done, I was soon to find out.

At the beginning or our trip, I went to Colombia's capital city of Bogota, in preparation for our outreach. Ricardo, our Colombian staff representative, was to accompany me to the main TV stations where we hoped to arrange for "Fury to Freedom" to be shown. After spending an entire day fighting traffic and being insulted, rejected, and ignored by television representatives and directors, I decided that we should shake the dust off our feet and leave Bogota.

There was one more station we hadn't tried. It was one of the biggest, so I figured they would surely turn us down. Ricardo, however, talked me into going. I was so disgusted that I actually didn't want them to have the privilege of hearing the gospel! When I went up to the information desk I spoke in English, hoping that no one would understand. The gentleman at the desk got very excited and dialed a number quickly.

"There is a woman here who cannot speak a word of Spanish. I think she's a producer from the U.S.A.!" he explained rapidly. Ricardo, who had studied in the United States and is perfectly bilingual, glanced at me and we both giggled at God's cleverness.

The next thing we knew, we were sitting in th' of one of the major directors of that network station, I had tried to evade telling the was about Christ and His changin in order to get their attention care! I blurted out the fac reluctantly started. I group on the other side of the steep mountains, down in the city of Villavicencio.

"This movie is what our country needs!" the man exclaimed. "Come back next week and we'll discuss the possibility of airing it." He talked as if we lived right around the corner.

Again, I learned that God and His people travel first-class. He won't settle for anything less. "Smooth sailing. . . ." I smiled.to myself. And so it was, until we found ourselves on the treacherous road that winds through the mountains, and sometimes slides down the hills and into the Colombian rivers.

Ricardo was to drive, and Alejandro, a recording music artist from our staff, was to serve as copilot. I made my bed in the backseat of the car, deciding to sleep the mountain ordeal out of existence. For some reason, hundreds of trucks decided to escort us that night. Our exhaust and the exhaust from their poorly maintained engines was so dense that it obscured our vision of the dense greenery, wild-growing orchids, hundreds of waterfalls and, thank God, the cliffs around each bend. Then, to my great discomfort, I began to react to the fumes. I didn't want to complain. After all, hadn't we been trained to endure hardship?

I   ' to black out, but I held my peace.

        'e window, but it made matters worse.

        get j was losing consciousness.

        'ease stop for a little bit? I feel kind

        g to minimize the problem.

        clearly worried.

        'ly green, Sharon.

        nd hands,

        ' to carry

        'ed me

        ing it

would help. It didn't. Desperation and sickness washed over me in immense waves. This road in itself was a death threat. If something happened to me, it would be impossible to get any help. Was this it for me?

Then somehow, between the blackouts, a verse I had learned as a little girl glimmered in my mind: "I will lift up mine eyes unto the hills, from whence cometh my help . . ." (Psalm 121:1).

I looked up. A full moon shone back at me in all its splendor and glory.

"God, I'm so sorry, but if I survive this, I don't ever want to travel this road again. I don't really care if the movie gets on TV or not. I don't have the courage to go on. What a flake I am! I'm sorry. Forgive me, please. If there's any other way, show me. But it can't involve this road. I know You understand. You're the only one who knows how I feel." I lay my head against the window and waited to pass out.

All at once my thoughts were stilled. Jesus' Gethsemane prayer came into my mind: "Oh my Father, if this cup [His death on the cross] may not pass away from me, except I drink it, thy will be done" (Matthew 26:42). I could just hear Jesus saying to me, "I know. I didn't want to hang on the cross either." He understood how I felt. What I was going through was nothing compared to what He had suffered.

"Thy will be done," I whispered.

Instantly I was healed. I no longer felt sick, and the fumes were no longer affecting me. I took a quick look in the mirror. My hair looked like a used mop and my makeup was smeared, but my cheeks were regaining their color.

"I'm okay, guys! Speed up! Let's get this show on the road. We have places to go, people to meet, movies to show. . . . I'm well! God's healed me!"

"Are you sure?" asked Alejandro.

"Of course I'm sure! It's my body and I can tell!"

The rest of the trip was trouble-free. And it was well worth the trouble it had caused. *Fury to Freedom* was the feature film on Colombian television the following Christmas Eve. Our missionary commitment was bearing fruit at last.

Not long after this threat upon my life, just as I was about to address a large group of women, I received an emergency call from Raul. "Debbie is dying." I couldn't believe my ears. After speaking, I drove home, weeping all the way.

"Father, please spare her life," I cried out, again and again.

"Why, God?" I asked.

When I got home, a verse from Song of Solomon answered my question: "My beloved [Jesus] spoke and said unto me [His bride], 'Rise up, my love, my fair one, and come away.' " Her eternal Groom was calling her home; her time on earth was over.

Debbie died two weeks later.

The casket was closed. I wouldn't have looked anyway. I wanted to remember her the way she looked the last time I saw her. We had been together on the beach in front of her house. She had stood looking out toward the ocean the whole time, not wanting to miss one glimpse of the sunset. Her wavy, dark-brown hair was blowing freely in the wind. She was a beautiful woman indeed.

There was a wide, white ribbon wrapped around the casket with the inscription "Steve Loves Debbie." Pictures of her and all her children were sitting on top of it. Behind stood a brand-new surfboard her husband and children had been planning to give her for Christmas.

Steve, her husband who had worked with us in the early days of our ministry, was now an assistant pastor at a sister fellowship near the beach. He performed Debbie's funeral himself, his voice trembling with every word: "On her finger she wore a ring with the inscription 'Jesus' on it." He struggled to continue. "You see, she belonged to Him."

I looked down at my hands; I wore one too.

Steve preceded to compare his wife to the virtuous woman who is described in Proverbs 31. I agreed with his description. But no other love, not even a love as deep as Steve's, had kept Debbie from the Master's hold on her life.

And now she was free at last—free from the body that had held her captive, free to spend eternity with her Husband, her Maker.

Debbie's death confirmed in my spirit the importance of placing our eyes on eternal values. Until the day of Jesus' return or my own death, I determined I would "lay up treasure in heaven." The fathers of our faith had their eyes focused on their eternal home. Even though all the desires of their hearts were not fulfilled in their lifetimes, they clung tenaciously to God's promises, confessing that they were strangers and pilgrims on the earth. "For [they] looked for a city which hath foundations, whose builder and maker is God."

I missed Debbie. My heart grieved for her husband, her lovely children, for all of us who remained behind. Although I was helpless to comfort her family, I was confident that God would be a mother to the children, and would meet Steve's emotional needs. I have learned that He is the All-Sufficient One, transforming Himself into whatever we require.

Jesus' words to His disciples comforted me, too:

> Let not your heart be troubled: ye believe in God, believe also in me. In my Father's house are many mansions: if it were not so, I would have told you. I go to prepare a place for you. And if I go . . . I will come again, and receive you unto myself; that where I am, there ye may be also (John 14:1-3).

Debbie looked forward to seeing her Lord, and she is with Him today. Someday my own longing for Him will be fulfilled. Someday He will come for me, too.

———————

Saturday morning arrived, and I hadn't seen Raul for two weeks. He'd promised me the day before that he would take me to the Queen Mary, a luxurious English passenger ocean liner that once proudly traveled the world's seas. Now she regally reigns in splendor over California's Long Beach Harbor, where thousands of international tourists examine her lavish dining halls, cabins, decks, and extravagant interiors.

The alarm rang. I woke up to a red rose and a note lying on my nightstand. "Sorry, Sharon. I forgot I had to speak at a conference today. Be back late. I know you understand. I love you, Raul."

At first I was angry, and pulled the blanket over my head. My thoughts raced. Shall I be depressed today? I could throw away the rose. But I no longer had my little green metal box where I had once stored all my love notes.

In yet another "living sacrifice" offering unto the Lord, I had burned its flattering contents in my fireplace. I had told God that I could be content with His love for me and would no longer need to hold on to those complimentary words, reaffirming man's approval.

I had made a wise choice then. Now I would make another. Why should I be depressed? I would visit the Queen Mary anyway. I would go with my Husband, my Maker.

"God, do You date?" I laughed at the silence.

"Of course You do. Let's go!" I jumped out of bed, showered, and dressed. I was determined to look gorgeous—for Him.

I drove with my Lord to the docks, ate lunch, bought myself a gift—and we thoroughly enjoyed the day. On the way out, I confidently walked along the deck, fully conscious of His company. I sensed a special glow about myself.

Now and then someone turned and looked my way. I wondered if they could see Him: my Captain—the One I travel with.

Happily Ever After...

Edited by Ann Warren

'... and so they got married and lived happily ever after.'

In these days of soaring divorce statistics, is this idea just a romantic dream? Is it possible for two people to meet, marry and stay loving each other for a lifetime?

Ten Christian women in the limelight talk frankly about the men they married - how more than waistline and hairline have changed since their wedding days. If you are wondering whether you have met the right person, you should read this real-life book first.

'Helpful and frank' - Women's Aglow Fellowship.

Bridget Plass, Sally McClung, Mary Reid, Annabel Crawley, Gill Brentford, Hazel Barclay, Anne Townsend, Gail Lawther, Valerie Griffiths and Ann Warren all tell their stories. Ann Warren, who compiled them, is a freelance writer and pastoral counsellor. After starting work in the BBC she was a regular contributor to Company (TVS), and served as a member of the General Synod. Ann and her husband Peter have travelled extensively in their twenty-six years of marriage.

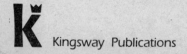

Kingsway Publications

Marriage As God Intended

by Selwyn Hughes

'We have never had an argument in the whole of our marriage,' said the husband.
'How did you accomplish that?' asked the counsellor.
'We just don't talk.'

Communication is only one of the problem areas faced by married couples—there can be many other difficulties that cause us to fall short of God's perfect plan.

This book offers help—not only with specific problems, but for improving what is already good and healthy.

There are chapters on:
> relationships with parents and in-laws
> who's the head of the family?
> sexual difficulties
> the temptation to adultery
> divorce and remarriage

Selwyn Hughes is highly respected as a leading marriage guidance counsellor. Here he draws on his many years' experience as both husband and counsellor, blending biblical principles with practical suggestions on how to let God keep your marriage at its best.

Kingsway Publications